LIFE IS IN THE BLOOD

Larry Ollison

For the life of the flesh is in the blood,
and I have given it to you upon the altar
to make atonement for your souls;
for it is the blood that makes atonement for the soul.
— Leviticus 17:11

Larry Ollison Ministries
Osage Beach, Missouri

Life is in the Blood
Published by:
Larry Ollison Ministries
P.O. Box 880
Osage Beach, MO 65065
ISBN 0-9653202-3-5

Cover design and book production by:
DB & Associates Design Group, Inc.
dba Double Blessing Productions
P.O. Box 52756, Tulsa, OK 74152
www.doubleblessing.com

Printed in the United States of America.

Dedication

From the first day the ink touched the paper, I knew this book was dedicated to Stan Moore. There are days that impact us and change the course of our lives. September 28, 1999 was such a day for me.

While attending a ministers' conference in Texarkana, Arkansas, hosted by Tracy Harris, I encountered a message that would mark and imprint me for life. Stan Moore, pastor of Words of Life Fellowship Church in Miami, Florida, was a featured speaker along with Terry Mize, Dennis Burke, Jerry and Carolyn Savelle and other great men and women of God.

I had never met Stan Moore before that day, but as this "elder statesman of God" took the platform, Loretta and I sat pierced by the message.

Although I was raised a Southern Baptist and had been taught about the "precious blood of Jesus" and "the blood shed on Calvary's tree," I had never heard the blood of Jesus taught this way. An explosion took place inside of me. I couldn't hear enough or read enough about the blood of Jesus. The Word became rhema. Pastor Stan and his lovely wife, Jeri, have set a standard of excellence and integrity and I consider it an honor to be their friend and co-worker in the ministry of Jesus Christ.

The "Word of Life" spoken by Pastor Stan Moore was the seed of inspiration that birthed this book.

Contents

Dedication

Acknowledgments

Forewords

Introduction

1. The Word, the Name, the Blood 1
2. Jesus — Our Substitute 11
3. The Significance of the Blood...................................27
4. Accessing the Power of the Blood 43
5. Understanding the New Covenant 59
6. How to Gain Access to the Promises of God 71
7. The Power to Stand 83
8. The Power to Defeat Sin 101
9. Jesus is the Door 115

How to Become a Christian

Acknowledgments

First and foremost I would like to give thanks to Alice McDermott. For over a year she has lovingly worked on this book. Her very life and personal ministry acknowledges the power of the blood of Jesus. Her heart has touched and examined every word in this manuscript. Thank you Jim, Christy and Darin for sharing your wife and mother with this project.

Thanks to Bev Herring for transcribing and framing the original manuscript. She truly is gifted.

Also, a special thanks to Stan Moore, Billye Brim and Loretta, my wife and partner in the ministry, for lending me your knowledge and research on the blood of Jesus. The three of you laid the foundation for and inspired this book. Thank you!

Forewords

It is an honor and a privilege to write a forward for two of my close friends in the ministry, Pastor Larry and Loretta Ollison. Larry's new book, Life is in the Blood, is required reading for those desiring to see the supernatural, wonder working, miracle power of God through the blood of Jesus Christ. The late Dr. Lester Sumrall has stated that the teaching on the blood is the most important subject in the Bible.

Our congregation at Words of Life Fellowship Church in Miami, Florida has experienced awesome miracles since 1994. We will continue to experience them as we continue to honor the blood by teaching, singing, talking and pleading the blood. When we honor the blood, the blood will honor us.

Pastor Stan Moore
Words of Life Fellowship Church
Miami, Florida

This book is the Breakfast of Champions! The book, Life is in the Blood, is a must-read for all Champions in Christ!

Life is in the Blood covers it all! It is a great tool for overcoming Satan and to continually keep him defeated. It is based on the scriptures that will help you in all areas of life and it shows you the principles you need to follow.

Through this book you will learn the importance of the blood of Jesus and the power that is found in that blood. Jesus did not just sacrifice His life to allow us entrance into heaven, even though that is a wonderful blessing, but He made a way for us to be protected and walk in victory here on this earth. He wants us to use this power that was given. He wants us to walk in this covenant that was made through His blood. He wants us to live in the promises that were given in this covenant.

In *Life is in the Blood,* we learn that our God is a covenant God that speaks and keeps His covenant. If it is written in His Word, then so be it! He is a God of goodness, mercy and love. God brought us the goodness of His love through the blood of Jesus. We have access to this covenant because of the blood!

We have been engrafted into a wonderful family, with Christ as our brother and God as our father! What a family! Many benefits come with this family and they are found in our covenant with Christ. In this book you will learn of our covenant with Christ and will walk in a closer relationship with Jesus allowing you to receive the promises that Jesus paid the price for with His precious blood!

Life is in the Blood is not just a nice name for a book, but a truth about the reality of the blood of Jesus! Life ***is*** in the ***blood***! The power to stand against anything that this world has to offer is in the blood. The power to defeat Satan and sin in our lives is in the blood! The power to control our flesh is in the blood! The power to live victoriously in life is in the blood!

We now have another source, along with my mom's book (*The Blood and the Glory,* Billye Brim), concerning the blood and its power in our lives. This book is a blessing to the body of Christ and should be read by all.

Chip and Candace Brim
Champions 4 Christ
Branson, Missouri

Introduction

The word "blood" is mentioned 424 times in the Bible, yet little has been taught on the subject. Yes, there are those who do understand the importance of the blood, but they are few. My desire is to change that.

This book is not intended to be an exhaustive study of the blood or the blood covenant. My desire is to build the foundation for the revelation knowledge of the supernatural blood of our Lord and Savior Jesus Christ and to fuel the thirst for depth in the Word.

Join me in my quest as we discover that "Life is in the Blood."

Chapter 1

The Word, the Name, the Blood

There are certain events that take place in our lives that change us. We can all look back to experiences in our lives that have made dramatic impacts on who we are. It could be when you got saved, or when you got filled with the Holy Spirit, or perhaps when you got married. As you read this book, I believe it also will be a life changing experience.

The Power of the Word

"The Word, the Name, the Blood" is the new theme at our church. Like many churches, we have majored on the power of the Word of God because it's the Word of God that sets us free. Jesus said in John 8:31,32, *"If you abide in My word...you shall know the truth and the truth shall set you free."* The Word of God can and will set you free. We know there's power in the Word of God.

The Power of the Name

We know there's power in the name of Jesus. When Peter and John were standing in front of the lame man in Acts chapter 3, they said to him, "In the name of Jesus, rise and walk." The man jumped up and leaped, totally healed.

The Word says Peter looked out at the crowd and asked them why they were so amazed. "It's not us. It's the power in the name." Then Peter went on to preach faith in the name of Jesus because he wanted them to know that it was Jesus Who had given this man strength and made him whole.

The name of Jesus is above every name that is named (Philippians 2:9). There is no name above the name of Jesus. Every name that is named has to bow to the name of Jesus. Cancer is a name and it has to bow to the name of Jesus. Diabetes is a name and it has to bow to the name of Jesus. Sickness, disease and poverty are just names and they all have to bow to the name of Jesus. The scripture tells us over and over and over again — it's by the name.

When Peter and John were arrested in Acts chapter 4, the religious leaders told them one thing. Quit preaching about that name! Don't speak the name.

There's power in the Word. There's power in the name.

The Power of the Blood

One teaching in the Bible that has been overlooked by many in the church is the power of the blood of Jesus. One major denomination put out a new version of the Bible a few years ago and omitted fifteen references to the blood of Jesus! Another major denomination decided their songs had too much about the blood, so they eliminated all songs in their hymnals which referred to the blood. Much of the religious community has the view that we are more civilized now and talking about blood is offensive.

The devil wants us to eliminate the blood from our theology so we will be powerless. A powerless Christian is easily defeated. A powerless Christian is easily deceived. A powerless Christian will easily fall into sin. Satan knows if he can deceive us into ignoring the blood, we will be overtaken.

As a believer you are the temple of the Holy Spirit. The Holy Spirit will not move into a vessel that's full of sin. When you were saved, you were made righteous by the blood of Jesus cleansing you from all unrighteousness (1 John 1:7). Without the blood cleansing you from all unrighteousness, the Spirit of God will not live in you and will not move through you.

Second Corinthians 5:17 says old things pass away and all things become new when we become born again. Water baptism represents the death of the old man and the resurrection (new birth) into new life. We symbolically bury our sin and the old man, and come up out of the water cleansed by the blood and reborn. No wonder the devil wants us to be ignorant about the blood of Jesus.

When you get saved, you are cleansed by the power of the blood and your sins are washed away, not just covered. You become a new creation in Christ and the Spirit of God moves into your heart. Life is in the blood. Genesis 9:4 says, *"But you shall not eat flesh with its life, that is, its blood."*

Leviticus 17:11 says, *"For the life of the flesh is in the blood, and I have given it to you upon the altar to make atonement for your souls; for it is the blood that makes atonement for your soul."* How much clearer could it be? The scripture says the life of the flesh is in the blood.

The words "atone" and "atonement" mean to cover. In the Old Testament the blood of bulls and goats covered the people's sin.

Living Under a Better Covenant

Let me give you an illustration. We have all seen the little red wagons that children play with. If you would take one of these wagons and fill it with dirt and decide you wanted the dirt hidden, you could cover the wagon and the dirt with a canvas. Using Old Testament terms, we could say the dirt was "atoned." But even though the dirt was covered, the reality is, it was still there. If the wind came along and blew the canvas off the wagon, the dirt (sin) would be exposed and would need to be covered again. It took works to cover the wagon and to keep it covered.

Under the new covenant, Jesus dumped the dirt out of the wagon and cleansed the wagon with His blood. No longer does the wagon need to be covered. The dirt is not there. The wagon is clean. Using New Testament terms, the wagon has been "made righteous." It is clean and cleansed and ready to be filled with the Holy Spirit.

In Old Testament times, they had to have a continual sacrifice of the blood of bulls and goats to atone for their sin. They still had their sins. They were just covered so God wouldn't have to look at them. That explains why the Holy Spirit did not reside permanently in the people of God under the old covenant, but can now literally live inside of the New Testament believer.

That's why Hebrews 8:6 tells us that the new covenant is better than the old covenant. Does that mean all sin is gone? Let's look into some scriptures for the answer.

We Renew Our Minds with the Word

When you study the Bible, you must be sure you are rightly dividing the Word. *"Be diligent to present yourself approved to God, a worker who does not need to be ashamed, rightly dividing the word of truth"* (2 Timothy 2:15). You need to understand who the scripture is talking to and the context in which it is said. Obviously, if you can rightly divide the Word of God, it must mean you can also wrongly divide it. Therefore, let's look closely at what the Bible says concerning how we are cleansed from sin.

First, we must understand that we are a three-part being. We are body, soul and spirit (1 Thessalonians 5:23). We are a spirit that has a soul that lives in a body. Putting it very simply, but generally speaking, that is how we function.

In 1 John 3:9 the scripture says, *"Whoever has been born of God does not sin, for His seed remains in him; and he cannot sin, because he has been born of God."* That is talking about your spirit.

The scripture does not say your soul — which is your mind, your will, your intellect and your reasoning — does not sin. It says your spirit does not sin. Your spirit has been cleansed and is renewed daily by God, but your soul is your responsibility. That is why the scriptures tell us that we must daily renew our minds and wash them in the water of the Word. As Christians we are responsible for the renewal of our minds. It is not automatic just because we are saved.

> **And do not be conformed to this world, but be transformed by the renewing of your mind, that you may prove what is that good and acceptable and perfect will of God.**
>
> **Romans 12:2**

> **Therefore we do not lose heart. Even though our outward man is perishing, yet the inward man is being renewed day by day.**
>
> **2 Corinthians 4:16**

While our spirit is headed in the right direction, we still have a battle going on in our minds over the bad thoughts that still want to live there. We must daily renew the mind through the washing of the Word. If we don't renew our minds, we will continue to think like the world, which is inspired by what the devil thinks.

God Renews Our Spirit with the Blood

The Lord gave Moses a law concerning the animals they ate which explains the importance of the blood.

> **For it** [the blood] **is the life of all flesh. Its blood sustains its life. Therefore I said to the children of Israel, 'You shall not eat the blood of any flesh, for the life of all flesh is in its blood...'**
>
> **Leviticus 17:14**

The scripture makes it clear how important the blood is. Life is sustained by blood. Life is atoned by blood. In John 6:54 Jesus makes an interesting statement. *"Whoever eats My flesh and drinks My blood has eternal life, and I will raise him up at the last day."* Jesus is saying that life is contained in His blood. Our spirits are sustained and kept alive by the blood of Jesus.

How to Overcome the Devil

Revelation 12:11 says, *"And they overcame him* [the devil] *by the blood of the Lamb and by the word of their testimony, and they did not love their lives to the death."* The scripture does not say they overcame him by their testimony only. It says they overcame him by the word of their testimony. The word of their testimony was the Word. They spoke the Word of God. It took two things to overcome the devil. It took the blood of the Lamb (Jesus) and the saints speaking the Word of God.

The way Jesus overcame Satan during His temptation was by using the Word. He said, "It is written."

> **And Jesus answered and said to him, "Get behind Me, Satan! For it is written, 'You shall worship the LORD your God, and Him only you shall serve.'"**
>
> **Luke 4:8**

We need to know about the Word, but we also need to understand that it takes the blood of the Lamb and the Word to overcome.

Is it possible that as New Testament Christians we can be correctly speaking the Word of God in the name of Jesus and not see results? What is our response when we do not see the results? Do we just speak the Word louder and start telling God how we are in faith and all we are doing for Him, when we're really missing the component of the blood? They overcame by the blood of the Lamb and by the Word of their testimony.

By hearing and confessing the Word and by being cleansed by the blood, we enter into salvation. The devil will do everything in his power to discredit the Word and devalue and dilute the blood.

> **And war broke out in heaven: Michael and his angels fought with the dragon; and the dragon and his angels fought,**
>
> **but they did not prevail, nor was a place found for them in heaven any longer.**
>
> **So the great dragon was cast out, that serpent of old, called the Devil and Satan, who deceives the whole world; he was cast to the earth, and his angels were cast out with him.**
>
> **Revelation 12:7-9**

The devil was cast to the earth and his angels with him. The scripture says he is a deceiver. He deceived one third of the heavenly host into thinking that somehow he could overthrow God. They believed in a lie. The devil works the same way today. You would think over the centuries men would have become wise to the lies of the devil. Many have, but many people continue to believe his lies.

> **You are of your father the devil, and the desires of your father you want to do. He was a murderer from the beginning, and does not stand in the truth, because there is no truth in him. When he speaks a lie, he**

speaks from his own resources, for he is a liar and the father of it.

John 8:44

We Are Not Angels

Let me clarify something here. There is no place in the scriptures that says believers are angels. Believers have never been angels, nor will we become angels when we die. When we die, we are not going to be like Jimmy Stewart in the movie, *It's a Wonderful Life,* dealing with somebody that's trying to get their wings by doing something good. This is Hollywood theology. We are not angels and never will be angels.

Likewise, God is not an angel, the Holy Spirit is not an angel and Jesus is not an angel. Jesus is not related to the devil. The devil is nothing more than a created angel who rose up and attempted to be like God and was cast out of heaven to earth just as the scripture said.

Satan and his band of renegade angels will all be cast into hell. Hell was not created for sinners, although lost people will go there. Hell was created for fallen angels including the devil.

Then He will also say to those on the left hand, "Depart from Me, you cursed, into the everlasting fire prepared for the devil and his angels."

Matthew 25:41

We have something that angels don't have. We have blood. Not only do we have our blood, we have access to the blood of Jesus which cleanses us from all unrighteousness. Angels cannot be where we are. The scripture says they look on and want to be where we are.

To them it was revealed that, not to themselves, but to us they were ministering the things which now have been reported to you through those who have preached the gospel to you by the Holy Spirit sent from heaven — things which angels desire to look into.

1 Peter 1:12

But they can't be where we are because we have been created in the likeness of God.

What Were We Saved From?

But God demonstrates His own love toward us, in that while we were still sinners, Christ died for us.

Much more then, having now been justified by His blood, we shall be saved from wrath through him.

Romans 5:8,9

The scripture says, "We shall." That means there's no way we won't be.

For all have sinned and fall short of the glory of God,

being justified freely by His grace through the redemption that is in Christ Jesus,

whom God set forth as a propitiation by His blood, through faith, to demonstrate His righteousness, because in His forbearance God had passed over the sins that were previously committed,

to demonstrate at the present time His righteousness, that He might be just and the justifier of the one who has faith in Jesus.

Romans 3:23-26

Verse 25 says, *"Whom God set forth as a propitiation."* Propitiation is another word for substitute. I don't know why the word "propitiation" is used instead of "substitute" because propitiation is not a word we use much in our English language. The scripture says God sent Jesus as a substitute.

I am so glad Jesus was my substitute because He was without sin. Because He died, I don't have to die spiritually. Because He took stripes on His body for my healing, I can be healed. In 2 Corinthians 8:9 it says, *"For you know the grace of our Lord Jesus Christ, that though He*

[Jesus] *was rich, yet for your sakes He became poor, that you through His poverty might become rich."* Because He became poor, I can be rich. That is exactly what the Word of God says. Isn't that a loving God? Jesus became our substitute. He died so we can live. It only requires that we have faith in the blood and He will become our substitute.

Christ has redeemed us from the curse of the law by His blood. Ephesians 1:7 says, *"In Him* [Jesus] *we have redemption through His blood, the forgiveness of sins...."* Without His blood there is no forgiveness of sins. Life is in the blood. Your blood is what carries the life that's within you. That's why the devil attacks through the blood. If you have a disease, the doctor will test your blood to see what disease is in it.

People with diabetes have to check their sugar levels. What do they check? They check their blood. When doctors are checking people for AIDS, they check their blood. Where is your life? The scripture says it is in the blood. If you have pure blood, you are going to be healthy because your life is in your blood.

Let me tell you something. Jesus was perfect — physically, spiritually, mentally. That is why the shedding of His blood was the perfect sacrifice.

As you understand the concept of the power of the blood, miracles will take place because there is protection in the blood of Jesus.

You do not have to allow the devil to come in. You can stand face to face with him until he moves. You do not have to put up with sickness, disease, accidents or poverty. The power of Jesus' blood is here for you today!

Chapter 2
Jesus — Our Substitute

In order to understand or have knowledge of the blood, we have to know about it. Jesus said in John 8:31-32, *"If you abide in My word, you are My disciples indeed. And you shall know the truth, and the truth shall make you free."*

Hosea 4:6 says, *"My people perish for a lack of knowledge."* It isn't someone else's people, but His people. God is telling us that unless we know the truth of His Word, we will perish. Jesus is the Word. Jesus is the Truth.

Some people don't like to dig into the scripture, verse by verse and line by line. It takes time and diligence. But the Bible says all scripture is profitable for us to learn from, so we must take the time to study and unlock the mysteries of God's Word. It just makes good sense to spend time understanding something that is going to profit us.

Our Justifier

We need to know we are redeemed from the curse of the law. The law is not gone, but we have been redeemed from the curse of it.

Romans chapter three says,

> **But now the righteousness of God has been revealed independently and altogether apart from law, although actually it is attested by the Law and the prophets,**

Namely, the righteousness of God which comes by believing with personal trust and confident reliance on Jesus Christ, the Messiah. [And it is meant] for all who believe. For there is no distinction,

Since all have sinned and are falling short of the honor and glory which God bestows and receives.

[All] are justified and made upright and in right standing with God, freely and gratuitously by His grace (His unmerited favor and mercy), through the redemption which is [provided] in Christ Jesus,

Whom God put forward [before the eyes of all] as a mercy seat and propitiation by His blood [the cleansing and life-giving sacrifice of atonement and reconciliation to be received] through faith. This was to show God's righteousness, because in His divine forbearance He had passed over and ignored former sins without punishment.

It was to demonstrate and prove at the present time (in the now season) that He Himself is righteous and that He justifies and accepts as righteous him who has [true] faith in Jesus.

Romans 3:21-26 (AMP)

In verse 25 we understand that Jesus is our propitiation or substitute. Jesus took the place of the shed blood of animals necessary to fulfill the Old Testament law. We have only to accept the blood by faith to no longer be held accountable for sin. In doing this, God proved His righteousness. It says in His "forbearance" He chose not to punish us for past sins.

Verse 26 says He further proves His righteousness by even now showing He is just by being the One who justifies us when we have faith in Jesus.

What Paul is saying in this scripture is that Jesus became our substitute by His blood. There are other scriptures that show us this same thing. In Ephesians 1:7, it says, *"In Him we have redemption through His blood..."* In other words, we have been redeemed.

What It Means to be Redeemed

Do you know what it's like to redeem something? Let me use an illustration. Let's say you take a prized possession down to the pawnshop. The guy at the pawnshop gives you $50 and a ticket for it and puts it on the shelf. As soon as you get $50 together, you can go back to the pawnshop, give him the ticket and the money, and you can get your possession back. You have "redeemed" it.

It's the same way with coupons. When you take a dollar coupon for cereal to the grocery store, you can redeem it toward the box of cereal. What you're actually doing is using it as a substitute for a dollar toward the purchase of the cereal.

Jesus redeemed us by paying the price we couldn't pay. He is our Redeemer. Look at the rest of Ephesians 1:7, *"In Him we have redemption through His blood, the forgiveness of sins, according to the riches of His grace."* In other words, "the riches of His grace" means that He has the ability to do through you the thing that you can't do. He is so rich in grace that He can provide enough grace for every single person to do the thing that they cannot do for themselves.

There is no earthly person who can pay the price for salvation. It does not matter how hard a person may work at it. People can do good deeds. They can tithe and have so many Sunday School pins hanging off the left side of their lapel that they walk crooked, but that will not get them saved. No one can be saved by works. Nothing, absolutely nothing you can do can save you. Romans 3:23 says, *"All have sinned and fall short of the glory of God."* There is nothing you can do to change that by yourself. Without the blood of Jesus you will die short of the glory of God.

However, if we look at Ephesians 1:7,8, it explains that, *"we have redemption through His blood, the forgiveness of sins, according to the riches of His grace which He made to abound toward us in all wisdom and prudence."* Wow, isn't that great? His grace abounds toward us. We are blessed because God favors us. God favors us because of grace. He gives us favor when we don't deserve it.

The Mystery Revealed

It gets even more exciting! If we read Ephesians 1:7-9, we learn *"... His grace which He made to abound toward us in all wisdom and prudence, having made known to us the mystery of His will...."*

Here in this scripture God says, *"He has made known to us the mystery of His will."* It is His desire to make known to us the mystery of His will. It may be a mystery to the world, but it is not a mystery to us because we have the revelation of the Word. The world does not have the revelation of the Word. You cannot have the revelation of the Word when you are in the world.

> **But as it is written: "Eye has not seen, nor ear heard, Nor have entered into the heart of man the things which God has prepared for those who love Him."**
>
> **But God has revealed them to us through His Spirit....**
>
> **1 Corinthians 2:9,10**

All the Spirit of God is going to tell an unbeliever is, "You need Jesus. You need the blood. You need the Name. You need the Word. You need to get saved." That's because the scripture says that no one comes to the Father except one be drawn.

No one can come to Me unless the Father who sent Me draws him; and I will raise him up at the last day.

John 6:44

There is only one way to the Father and that is through Jesus.

Jesus said to him, "I am the way, the truth, and the life. No one comes to the Father except through Me."

John 14:6

Once you get saved, all of the mystery is available. It is available to any Christian who is willing to read the manual. Before you get saved, the deep mysteries of God will always be mysteries. But after salvation, revelation of the mysteries is available. Once we accept Jesus as our Lord and Savior, the veil over the Word is removed and through study and meditation the thing that was once a mystery now comes to light.

And He said to them, "To you it has been given to know the mystery of the kingdom of God; but to those who are outside, all things come in parables."

Mark 4:11

But the natural man does not receive the things of the Spirit of God, for they are foolishness to him; nor can he know them, because they are spiritually discerned.

1 Corinthians 2:14

Having made known to us the mystery of His will, according to His good pleasure which He purposed in Himself,

that in the dispensation of the fullness of the times He might gather together in one all things in Christ, both which are in heaven and which are on earth — in Him.

Ephesians 1:9,10

Predestination Explained

In Him also we have obtained an inheritance, being predestined according to the purpose of Him who works all things according to the counsel of His will.

Ephesians 1:11

The word "predestined" has confused many people for many years, but it is not really that difficult to understand. Here's a simple illustration of what it means to be predestined. If I'm preaching one Sunday and I take five one hundred dollar bills out of my pocket and ask for five people to come and each get one, I'm going to get five people on the platform in a hurry. I predetermined that whoever came up would receive a one hundred dollar bill from me. So, you could say they were predestined to be there because I knew they would come. I didn't know exactly who would come, but it was predestined or predetermined before the service that I was going to give away five one hundred dollar bills.

So, who came? It was those who answered the call. I chose to give the bills to whoever accepted and received the call. *"Many are called, but few are chosen"* (Matthew 22:14). Predestination shouldn't be confusing. Salvation is predestined for anyone who will walk forward and receive it.

Remember, in verse 11 it says, *"In Him also we have obtained an inheritance, being predestined according to the purpose of Him who works all things according to the counsel of His will."* It's that simple.

Understanding the Curse of the Law

The law itself is not a curse. It is a blessing. When Moses received the law from God, the Hebrews had just come out of Egypt. As a nation they had few rules and regulations to protect them. God's law as given to

Moses would help maintain an abundant and blessed lifestyle for all who would follow the law. It was only a curse to the disobedient.

The purpose of the law is to protect. Speed limits on the highway are a law. They are a blessing to those who drive the speed limit safely and a curse to those who disobey the speed limit and have an accident. Blessings and safety come through obedience. Destruction comes through disobedience.

In order to understand the curse of the law, we have to refer back to the Old Testament where it was given. The curse of the law as described in the New Testament, is usually referring to the blessings and cursings described in the first five books of the Old Testament: Genesis, Exodus, Leviticus, Numbers and Deuteronomy, also known as the Pentateuch. These five books, specifically Deuteronomy chapter 28, list blessings for obeying the law and curses for disobeying the law. Curses were not in existence until man separated himself from God in the Garden of Eden through disobedience.

When Adam and Eve sinned, their separation from God's provision brought them poverty, sickness, and spiritual death. In their own strength, there was no way out.

From Adam and Eve until the sacrifice of Christ, people were under the curse of poverty, sickness, and spiritual death. There was no way man could pay the price for healing, poverty or spiritual death. The law required a perfect sacrifice and no man was perfect. God had made a way through the law where the priest could cover sin by the blood sacrifice of animals. Once a year he would go into the Holy of Holies and the presence of God. The priests also offered daily sacrifices for the atoning or covering of the people's sins during the year. The ritual was long and had to be carefully executed.

Jesus came to earth and became our substitute sacrifice that, once and for all, broke the curse of the law. Jesus was the perfect sacrifice which broke the curse of the law for all who believe.

Jesus did more than atone. The word "atonement" means "to cover." Jesus cleansed us of our sins. He remitted our sins and He made reconciliation between man and God. Once He redeemed us from the debt we couldn't pay, it allowed the cleansed, born-again believer into the Holy of Holies and the presence of God. That is what the blood of Jesus did.

Jesus is Not Our Atonement

At this point, before we go any further in this book, I need to make one point perfectly clear. In order to understand this, I'm going to ask you to put away any denominational doctrines and look for a moment at the Word of God carefully and without prejudice.

Jesus is not our atonement. Your favorite song may say He is, but the Word of God does not say He is. In the King James Version the word "atonement" only occurs once in the New Testament in Romans 5:11. The same word translated "atonement" in this verse is translated "reconciliation" in other places. We must understand clearly that under the old covenant, sin was only covered. But under the new covenant, sin was eliminated. To say Jesus' blood atoned for our sins is belittling its value. His blood cannot be compared with the blood of animals because it did so much more.

The old covenant was only a shadow of the things to come, but the new covenant was the substance. Under the old covenant sacrifices were recurring; but under the new covenant the sacrifice was eternal. Under the old covenant lambs could only cover sin. But under the new covenant Jesus took away sin (John 1:29).

> **Who do not need daily, as those high priests, to offer up sacrifices, first for His own sins and then for the people's, for this He did once for all when He offered up Himself.**
>
> **Hebrews 7:27**

There is no covering for sin under the new covenant because there is no need for one. Jesus is not our atonement. He did away with our need for atonement. Where there is no sin, there is no need to cover sin.

The Blood is Our Protection!

> **And you shall take a bunch of hyssop, dip it in the blood that is in the basin, and strike the lintel and the two door posts with the blood that is in the basin. And none of you shall go out of the door of his house until morning.**
>
> **For the Lord will pass through to strike the Egyptians; and when He [the Lord] sees the blood on the lintel and on the two door posts, the Lord will pass over the door and not allow the destroyer to come into your houses to strike you.**
>
> **Exodus 12:22-23**

If you look carefully, you will see that in verse 23, the scripture says, *"the Lord will pass over the door and not allow the destroyer to come into your houses to strike you."* It is the blood that protects you. We are still under a blood covenant. If you think the blood covenant only applied to the physical sons of Abraham, look at Galatians 3:7:

> **Therefore know that only those who are of faith are sons of Abraham.**
>
> **Galatians 3:7**

We are people of faith. We have been saved by grace through faith (Ephesians 2:8). We just don't use the blood of bulls and goats anymore. We use the blood of Jesus. If the blood of sacrificial lambs had the kind of power that stopped the destroyer, how much more will the blood of Jesus protect you when it is applied to your household!

Eternal Life, Health and Prosperity

Jesus became our substitute and redeemed us from the whole curse of the law. The curse basically consisted of three parts.

The curse:

1) Spiritual death

2) Sickness and disease

3) Poverty

The redemption:

1) Eternal life (Hebrews 9:12)

2) Health and healing (1 Peter 2:24)

3) Prosperity (2 Corinthians 8:9)

Unfortunately, many people stop after one third of the curse has been broken in their life. Jesus paid the price to break the entire curse of the law, which included poverty, sickness, and spiritual death. We are good at telling people they need to become spiritually alive. We even tell them that when Jesus died on the cross, He became a curse (Galatians 3:13) and because He was cursed, we're not cursed anymore.

Why stop there? What about the curse of sickness and disease? What about the curse of poverty? He became our substitute in those things, too. The scripture clearly tells us so. He paid the price you couldn't pay so that you can be rich.

He took the curse of poverty for you and He paid the price. Second Corinthians 8:9 says, *"For you know the grace of our Lord Jesus Christ, that though He was rich, yet for your sakes He became poor, that you through His poverty might become rich."*

This scripture can only mean that Jesus was the substitute for your poverty. He was the propitiation for that part of the curse of the law for you.

One time I heard a preacher say, "I don't want to use the word 'rich.' I'm just going to say 'doing well.'" Is it wrong to quote the Bible? Some denominations don't want to use the word "blood" because they're afraid it's offensive. Other denominations don't want to use the word "rich" because it's offensive. Who decides which words we take out of the Bible and which ones we don't?

I believe if you are healthy, spiritually alive and you've got some money in the bank, you can do more for the Gospel than if you're lying on your back in a hospital with a dead spirit and you're dead broke.

The devil does not want you living the Gospel. The scripture says, *"For this purpose the Son of God was manifested, that He might destroy the works of the devil"* (1 John 3:8). What are the works of the devil? In John 10:10, Jesus tells us, *"The thief does not come except to steal, and to kill, and to destroy...."* Sounds like the curse of the law to me. The devil wants to kill you. He wants you spiritually dead. He wants to steal from you. He wants to destroy your body. The devil wants you to live under the curse. Jesus shed His blood so you wouldn't have to live under the curse.

Abundant Wealth — Abundant Health

In the rest of John 10:10, Jesus said, *"I have come that they may have life, and that they may have it more abun-*

dantly." As for me, I've had nothing and I've had a lot. I've been sick and I've been well. And I'll tell you what I think. Being well with money is a whole lot more fun than being sick with nothing. The choice is up to us. The scripture says, *"...I have set before you life and death, blessing and cursing. Therefore, choose life..."* (Deuteronomy 30:19). What more do we need to convince us? We have been redeemed from the curse of the law, the curse of poverty and the curse of sickness.

It was prophesied in Isaiah 53 that the Messiah would suffer on our behalf. In verse 5 it says, *"...And by His stripes we are healed."* In Matthew chapter 8 the scripture in Isaiah 53 is fulfilled:

> **When evening had come, they brought to Him many who were demon possessed. And He cast out the spirits with a word, and healed all who were sick,**
>
> **that it might be fulfilled which was spoken by Isaiah the prophet, saying: "He Himself took our infirmities and bore our sicknesses."**
>
> **Matthew 8:16,17**

We also see Isaiah 53 quoted in 1 Peter 2:24, but there it is looking back on the prophecy: *"Who Himself bore our sins in His own body on the tree, that we, having died to sins, might live for righteousness — by whose stripes you were healed."*

"Bore our sins" is in the past tense. It says *"were healed"* because we were healed when He bore the stripes for us. Isaiah was looking forward; 1 Peter 2:24 was looking back. It has already happened. That means Jesus paid the price! He paid the price for eternal life, healing and prosperity — all three parts of the curse of the law.

In Romans chapter 3, it says clearly how He paid the price. He did it by His blood. Without the blood of Jesus, we do not have everlasting life. Without the blood of Jesus, we do not have healing. Without the blood of Jesus, all we have is poverty. The blood of the Lamb redeemed us from all of these things, and He is the Lamb.

The Proof is in the Word

Let me give you some scriptures that are going to knock your socks off, if you happen to be wearing socks. In Genesis 2:17 it says, *"...In the day that you shall eat of it you shall surely die."* This scripture foretells that spiritual death will come upon man.

In John 3:4-6, Jesus told Nicodemus he had to be born again in order to have everlasting life. Look at Romans 8:2, *"For the law of the Spirit of life in Christ Jesus has made me free from the law of sin and death."* So Jesus has redeemed us and made us free from death. We are redeemed from the curse of spiritual death.

John 5:24 shows us how we passed from death to life. Jesus said, *"Most assuredly, I say to you, he who hears My word and believes in Him who sent Me has everlasting life, and shall not come into judgment, but has passed from death into life."* We shall not come into judgment! We passed from death to life! Here we are right at 2000 years after Jesus hung on the cross, shed His precious blood and all we have to do is accept what He paid for.

Jesus was God, but He came to earth as man. He was the Son of Man. When He came out of the grave He had defeated sin, death and the devil. He became the firstfruits of the kingdom (1 Corinthians 15:20). That's why He could take His rightful position as head of the church. We are each a part of His body.

We have this position in the body of Christ because we were brought back into spiritual fellowship by the blood. Ephesians 2:13 says, *"But now in Christ Jesus you who once were far off have been brought near by the blood of Christ."* Colossians 1:19-20, *"For it pleased the Father that in Him all the fullness should dwell, and by Him to reconcile all things to Himself, by Him, whether things on earth or in heaven, having made peace through the blood of His cross."*

Look at what it says in Hebrews chapter 2:

> **Inasmuch then as the children have partaken of flesh and blood, He Himself likewise shared in the same, that through death He might destroy him who had the power of death, that is, the devil,**
>
> **and release those who through fear of death were all their lifetime subject to bondage.**
>
> **For indeed He does not give aid to angels, but He does give aid to the seed of Abraham.**
>
> **Hebrews 2:14-16**

First, it says Jesus became like man and through His death destroyed the power of the devil! Remember we are the seed of Abraham because we are of faith. The scripture says God favors us so much (verse 16) that He will give aid to us when He will not give aid to angels. That almost sounds impossible, but the Word of God says it.

In Hebrews 9:11-14 it says:

> **But Christ came as High Priest of the good things to come, with the greater and more perfect tabernacle not made with hands, that is, not of this creation.**
>
> **Not with the blood of goats and calves, but with His own blood He entered the Most Holy Place once for all, having obtained eternal redemption.**
>
> **For if the blood of bulls and goats and the ashes of a heifer, sprinkling the unclean, sanctifies for the purifying of the flesh,**

how much more shall the blood of Christ, who through the eternal Spirit offered Himself without spot to God, cleanse your conscience from dead works to serve the living God?

Hebrews 9:11-14

Hebrews 9:24 says Christ didn't enter the Holy of Holies where the earthly priests went.

For Christ, the Messiah, has not entered into a sanctuary made with [human] hands, only a copy and pattern and type of the true one, but [He has entered] into heaven itself, now to appear in the [very] presence of God on our behalf.

Nor did He [enter into the heavenly sanctuary to] offer Himself regularly again and again, as the high priest enters the [Holy of] Holies every year with blood not his own;

For then would He often have had to suffer, [over and over again] since the foundation of the world. But as it now is, He has once for all at the consummation and close of the ages appeared to put away and abolish sin by His sacrifice [of Himself].

And just as it is appointed for [all] men once to die and after that the [certain] judgment,

Even so it is that Christ having been offered to take upon Himself and bear as a burden the sins of many once and once for all, will appear a second time, not carrying any burden of sin nor to deal with sin, but to bring to full salvation those who are (eagerly, constantly and patiently) waiting for and expecting Him.

Hebrews 9:24-28 (AMP)

Look at what these scriptures are saying. The high priest had to offer blood in the Holy of Holies on a yearly basis. Jesus took His own blood and went into the Holy of Holies, the real Holy of Holies in heaven — not the imitation down here. He went into the presence of God for us to put away our sin by the sacrifice of

Himself. Jesus was the perfect sacrifice. His blood did away with sin once and for all. He bore the sins of many — that is for all of us who believe. When we see Him again He will be apart from sin. Sin is gone — done away with completely.

The devil thought he had killed Jesus, but verse 26 tells us it was *"by the sacrifice of Himself."* If the devil had known what was going to happen when Jesus laid down His life, he and the demon hosts wouldn't have crucified Him. First Corinthians 2:8 says, *"Which none of the rulers of this age knew; for had they known, they would not have crucified the Lord of glory."* Satan is afraid of the blood. He would have never killed Jesus if He had known what the blood would do. That is why we must understand the significance of Jesus' blood.

Chapter 3

The Significance of the Blood

A relatively famous gentleman, who has his own program on cable television, called me one day. This man hangs around with movie stars and well-known figures from the sports world. However, he found out after all these years that wine, women and wealth couldn't give him peace, so he dialed the man of God. He was hungry for something that would give him real peace of mind. He realized there was something that would set him free that money couldn't buy.

Nothing but the Blood

And if you call on the Father, who without partiality judges according to each one's work, conduct yourselves throughout the time of your stay here in fear;

knowing that you were not redeemed with corruptible things, like silver or gold, from your aimless conduct received by tradition from your fathers,

but with the precious blood of Christ, as of a lamb without blemish and without spot.

1 Peter 1:17-19

There is the idea in the world that somehow silver and gold can purchase peace and redemption.

Nothing could be further from the truth. Prosperity will not redeem us. It doesn't mean we're not supposed to have it, or that prosperity is not a blessing for Christians to enjoy. In the same way, verse 18 says you can't be redeemed through the aimless conduct received by tradition from your fathers either. Just because your daddy or granddaddy went to Old Mount Zion Tabernacle Church and you've gone to every function in that church for forty years, that is not going to redeem you. Religious traditions cannot save you, nor will they bring peace.

The Word of God clearly states how we receive salvation in 1 Peter 1:19, *"But with the precious blood of Christ, as of a lamb without blemish and without spot."* Corruptible things like silver and gold or the aimless conduct of tradition will not redeem us. Redemption only comes through the precious blood of Jesus.

The word precious is not interpreted as we might commonly use it as "a precious little thing." The "precious" blood of Jesus means that His blood was costly.

Psalm 116:15 says, *"Precious in the sight of the LORD is the death of His saints."* When a saint dies of cancer or in a car wreck, it is very costly to the body of Christ. The body of Christ pays a price because there is one less Christian ministering the Gospel of Jesus Christ on the earth. The Amplified Bible defines the word precious in Psalm 116:15 as "important and no light matter."

The blood of Jesus was very costly. All through the New Testament, the scriptures make it clear there was a price paid for redemption. Jesus paid the ultimate price for us. It cost God the lifeblood of His only Son.

God Knows Things He Didn't Cause

He indeed was foreordained before the foundation of the world, but was manifest in these last times for you

who through Him believe in God, who raised Him from the dead and gave Him glory, so that your faith and hope are in God.

1 Peter 1:20,21

1 Peter 1:20 says, Jesus was foreordained before the foundation of the world. The Amplified Bible says, *"...He was chosen and foreordained (destined and foreknown for it) before the foundation of the world."* That means that even before the beginning in Genesis, God had appointed Jesus to shed His blood for our sins. Just because God knows about something, doesn't mean He causes it to happen. God did not cause Satan to rebel. God did not cause man to sin. God knew Lucifer would rise up and take one third of the heavenly host with him. And He knew that man would sin in the Garden of Eden. God knows everything that happens before it happens, but that doesn't mean He is the cause or that what happens is His will.

We may not understand why certain things happen because our minds are not as big as the mind of God. We have limited thinking. God knew He was going to send Jesus to shed His blood on the cross and redeem man. He knew that, even before man sinned, but He didn't cause man to sin. There is a big difference between looking down through the corridors of time and knowing something and being the cause of it.

So this is not meant to be interpreted as though God predestined man to sin. God, in His omniscience, saw ahead and as it states in verse 20, *"He*

[Jesus] *indeed was foreordained before the foundation of the world, but was manifest in these last times for you."*

Jesus was foreordained to shed His blood, and now Peter says, it has been made manifest. That means what was foreordained has happened as God said it would. We have been redeemed from sin.

First Peter 1:21 says, *"Who through Him believe in God, who raised Him from the dead and gave Him glory..."*

Why was Jesus given glory? Verse 21 continues to say *"...so that your faith and hope are in God."*

Because of the glory He received, we can have our faith and hope in God. Our hope and faith is our belief of what is coming and what we already have. They allow us to have a firm foundation of belief because of what Jesus did.

A Physical Copy of the Spiritual

For Christ has not entered the holy places made with hands, which are copies of the true, but into heaven itself, now to appear in the presence of God for us.

Hebrews 9:24

The Bible says Jesus entered the holy place not made with hands. Remember when God told Moses to build the tabernacle in the book of Exodus? God gave Moses specific measurements about how to make the Ark of the Covenant, and how to put the utensils in certain places, including exactly how thick and wide the veil was to be. Why do you think God was so specific? It's because these things already existed in the spirit realm and God was instructing man how to make the exact copies here on earth.

Who serve the copy and shadow of the heavenly things, as Moses was divinely instructed when he was about to make the tabernacle. For He said, "See that you make all things according to the pattern shown you on the mountain."

Hebrews 8:5

God wants to teach us by having us look at the physical copy of the original that already exists in the spirit realm. He knew when we move from the physical (copy) to the spiritual (original), we would already be familiar with it and understand.

Remember Hebrews 9:24 states, *"For Christ has not entered the holy places made with hands, which are copies of the true, but into heaven itself, now to appear in the presence of God for us."*

This scripture says Jesus did not enter the Holy of Holies that was made here on earth where the priests entered for the people. Jesus went into the Holy of Holies that is in the presence of God in heaven. The next verses of Hebrews 9 tell us why.

Not that He should offer Himself often, as the high priest enters the Most Holy Place every year with the blood of another —

He then would have to suffer often since the foundation of the world; but now, once at the end of the ages, He has appeared to put away sin by the sacrifice of Himself.

Hebrews 9:25,26

The scripture says if Jesus had gone into the copy or earthly tabernacle as the priest did when he took the blood of bulls and goats, then Jesus would also have had to continually come to sacrifice Himself. Instead of the priest ridding the people of their sin-consciousness every year, they were reminded of their sin and became more sin-conscious.

Hebrews 10:4 says, *"For it is not possible that the blood of bulls and goats could take away sins."* The blood of bulls and goats only covered the sin. Only the blood of Jesus took away the sin completely forever.

Where there is no sin, there no longer remains a reason to have sacrifices. The only reason for needing sacrifices would be if Jesus' blood didn't completely get rid of all the sin. Since His blood did redeem us from sin completely, there no longer remains a reason for an earthly blood sacrifice.

Hebrews 10:18,19 says, *"Now where there is remission of these, there is no longer an offering for sin. Therefore, brethren, having boldness to enter the Holiest by the blood of Jesus."* We can enter into the Holy of Holies now because we are without sin, because the blood of Jesus has cleansed us from all unrighteousness.

Once and For All

When Jesus went into the spiritual Holy of Holies and put His blood on the mercy seat, He was glorified. In the same way that it is appointed for man to die once and then the judgment, Jesus went in and made the ultimate sacrifice with His blood once, and it was done forever.

> **And as it is appointed for men to die once, but after this the judgment,**
>
> **so Christ was offered once to bear the sins of many. To those who eagerly wait for Him He will appear a second time, apart from sin, for salvation.**
>
> **Hebrews 9:27,28**

Why does it say apart from sin? Because upon entering the holy place, Jesus bore all our sins, but when we see Him again, He'll be apart from sin. Our sins no longer exist!

First John 1:7 says, *"But if we walk in the light as He is in the light, we have fellowship with one another, and the blood of Jesus Christ His Son cleanses us from all sin."* It doesn't say the sin is hidden or pushed to the side. We're cleansed from all sin, completely cleansed.

The Bible even provides a parallel between the spiritual and the physical. It's in Leviticus chapter 16.

> **And he shall take from the congregation of the children of Israel two kids of the goats as a sin offering, and one ram as a burnt offering.**
>
> **Aaron shall offer the bull as a sin offering, which is for himself, and make atonement for himself and for his house.**
>
> **He shall take the two goats and present them before the LORD at the door of the tabernacle of meeting.**
>
> **Then Aaron shall cast lots for the two goats: one lot for the LORD and the other lot for the scapegoat.**
>
> **And Aaron shall bring the goat on which the Lord's lot fell, and offer it as a sin offering.**
>
> **But the goat on which the lot fell to be the scapegoat shall be presented alive before the LORD, to make atonement upon it, and to let it go as the scapegoat into the wilderness.**
>
> **And Aaron shall bring the bull of the sin offering, which is for himself, and make atonement for himself and for his house, and shall kill the bull as the sin offering which is for himself.**

Then he shall take a censer full of burning coals of fire from the altar before the LORD, with his hands full of sweet incense beaten fine, and bring it inside the veil.

And he shall put the incense on the fire before the LORD, that the cloud of incense may cover the mercy seat that is on the Testimony, lest he die.

He shall take some of the blood of the bull and sprinkle it with his finger on the mercy seat on the east side; and before the mercy seat he shall sprinkle some of the blood with his finger seven times.

Then he shall kill the goat of the sin offering, which is for the people, bring its blood inside the veil, do with that blood as he did with the blood of the bull, and sprinkle it on the mercy seat and before the mercy seat.

So he shall make atonement for the Holy Place, because of the uncleanness of the children of Israel, and because of their transgressions, for all their sins; and so he shall do for the tabernacle of meeting which remains among them in the midst of their uncleanness.

Leviticus 16:5-16

There were four basic things that happened when the earthly priest made sacrifice on the Day of Atonement.

1) There was the sin offering for the priest himself.

2) There was the casting of lots between two goats.

3) The chosen goat was sacrificed.

4) The other goat was released into the wilderness as the scapegoat for the sins of the people. The word "scapegoat" we use today is actually a biblical term.

In the Old Testament, God gave Moses the procedure found in Leviticus chapter 16. Therefore, Jesus was required to shed His blood for the remission of the sins He carried for us. But on the third day, Jesus, the sinless priest, did what the Levitical priests could never do. He carried His blood into the heavenly Holy of Holies where it was accepted as the sacrificial blood, once and for all.

Notice in verse 13, it says if Aaron (or any priest) didn't perform the ritual in the manner God ordained it, he was a dead man. Dealing with sin was a life and death situation. The things God told the children of Israel to do were types and shadows of what was to come.

The Importance of the Glory

In John 20:15, Jesus had been resurrected, but He hadn't ascended to the Father. People were still figuring out that He was no longer in the tomb. When Mary saw Jesus, she thought He was the gardener. Study closely these next three verses.

> **Jesus said to her, "Woman, why are you weeping? Whom are you seeking?" She, supposing Him to be the gardener, said to Him, "Sir, if You have carried Him away, tell me where you have laid Him, and I will take Him away."**
>
> **Jesus said to her, "Mary!" She turned and said to Him, "Rabboni!" (which is to say, Teacher).**
>
> **Jesus said to her, "Do not cling to Me, for** [or because] **I have not yet ascended to My Father; but go to My brethren and say to them, 'I am ascending to My Father and your Father, and to My God and to your God.'"**
>
> **John 20:15-17**

Here's the situation. Jesus was barely out of the tomb when Mary showed up. However, she didn't recognize Him. When she did, she evidently started to touch Him. The Living Bible says that Jesus said, "Don't touch me...for I haven't yet ascended to My Father...."

Here is an important point we must not miss. Jesus had descended into the grave. Although He was resurrected when He saw Mary, He had not yet ascended to the throne and placed His blood on the mercy seat. When He put His blood on the mercy seat in the true Holy of Holies, not the one made with human hands, He came back to earth in His renewed, touchable body. He had been glorified in the same way we will be glorified. He then taught for forty days before His final ascension into heaven as described in the first chapter of Acts. This is why in Luke 24, it says:

> **Now as they said these things, Jesus Himself stood in the midst of them, and said to them, "Peace to you."**
>
> **But they were terrified and frightened, and supposed they had seen a spirit.**
>
> **And He said to them, "Why are you troubled? And why do doubts arise in your hearts?**
>
> **"Behold My hands and My feet, that it is I Myself. Handle Me and see, for a spirit does not have flesh and bones as you see I have."**
>
> **When He said this, He showed them His hands and His feet.**
>
> **Luke 24:36-40**

He urged them to openly handle Him so they would believe that He was not a spirit. This was after

Mary had seen Him and He had ascended into the true Holy of Holies and placed His blood on the mercy seat.

The Curse is Dead

The scriptures tell us that thorns were the result of a cursed earth. From the time Adam and Eve were driven out of the garden and told they could not enter in again, the ground produced thorns because it was cursed.

> **Then to Adam He said, "Because you have heeded the voice of your wife, and have eaten from the tree of which I commanded you, saying, 'You shall not eat of it': Cursed is the ground for your sake; in toil you shall eat of it all the days of your life.**
>
> **"Both thorns and thistles it shall bring forth for you, and you shall eat the herb of the field."**
>
> **Genesis 3:17,18**

> **For indeed they are gone because of destruction. Egypt shall gather them up; memphis shall bury them. Nettles shall possess their valuables of silver; thorns shall be in their tents.**
>
> **Hosea 9:6**

Jesus came to release us from the curse of the law. The curse of the law included every curse known to man. Let me show you what I mean. In Mark 15 it says:

> **So Pilate, wanting to gratify the crowd, released Barabbas to them; and he delivered Jesus, after he had scourged Him, to be crucified.**
>
> **Then the soldiers led Him away into the hall called Praetorium, and they called together the whole garrison.**
>
> **And they clothed Him with purple; and they twisted a crown of thorns, put it on His head,**

and began to salute Him, "Hail, King of the Jews!"

Then they struck Him on the head with a reed and spat on Him; and bowing the knee, they worshiped Him.

And when they had mocked Him, they took the purple off Him, put His own clothes on Him, and led Him out to crucify Him.

Mark 15:15-20

In John 19:5, there is another line added to this story. *"Then Jesus came out, wearing the crown of thorns and the purple robe. And Pilate said to them, 'Behold the Man!'"*

Since all scripture is profitable (2 Timothy 3:16), I propose to you that the crown of thorns, too, was a foreshadow. Nothing happened to Jesus accidently. When Jesus was put into the purple robe, even though the soldiers placed it on him mockingly, it represented His divine kingship.

While Jesus was taking a beating for us, He was removing the curse of sickness and disease. 1 Peter 2:24 says, *"...By whose stripes you were healed."* It was all done through the blood. It's because of His blood we have healing. There would be no healing without Jesus' blood. Jesus became our substitute. When the soldiers drove the nails through His flesh, He shed His precious blood for the remission of our sins.

I propose that when the thorns were pressed into His head, the blood of Jesus touching those thorns broke the curse of poverty for us. The lush conditions of Eden were restored.

When Jesus came back to restore things to the condition before the fall, He set it up so we could live in the fullness that was intended for God's children. He did more than give us everlasting life. He did more than just take away our sickness and disease. He became poor, so we could be rich. He redeemed us from the curse of the ground so we can live in an abundant harvest. It was paid for by Jesus' blood. Hebrews 6:7,8 refers to the thorns of the curse mentioned in Genesis 3.

> **For the earth which drinks in the rain that often comes upon it, and bears herbs useful for those by whom it is cultivated, receives blessing from God;**
>
> **but if it bears thorns and briars, it is rejected and near to being cursed, whose end is to be burned.**
>
> **Hebrews 6:7,8**

If they hadn't put the crown of thorns on Jesus' head, His blood wouldn't have touched the thorns and broken the curse. But they did! And we've been set free indeed!

The scripture tells us that if the princes of this earth had known what was going to happen when they crucified Jesus, they would never have done it.

> **Which none of the rulers of this age knew; for had they known, they would not have crucified the Lord of glory.**
>
> **1 Corinthians 2:8**

If they had known what putting a crown of thorns on His head and mocking Him as a king would do, they wouldn't have done it.

> **Son of man, speak to the children of your people, and say to them: "When I bring the sword upon a land, and the people of the land take a man from their territory and make him their watchman,**

"when he sees the sword coming upon the land, if he blows the trumpet and warns the people,

"then whoever hears the sound of the trumpet and does not take warning, if the sword comes and takes him away, his blood shall be on his own head."

Ezekiel 33:2-4

If we believe Jesus is our substitute and we heed the Word of God, then our blood will not be on our head because Jesus has already taken blood on His head for us.

The Blessings of Atonement and Redemption

Leviticus 14:14-18 foreshadows what Jesus did for us. Just as the priests performed the ritual explained earlier in Leviticus 8:23 before they could enter the Holy of Holies, these verses show how the same procedure was performed on an Israelite who came to him for atonement.

The priest shall take some of the blood of the trespass offering, and the priest shall put it on the tip of the right ear of him who is to be cleansed, on the thumb of his right hand, and on the big toe of his right foot.

And the priest shall take some of the log of oil, and pour it into the palm of his own left hand.

Then the priest shall dip his right finger in the oil that is in his left hand, and shall sprinkle some of the oil with his finger seven times before the Lord.

And of the rest of the oil in his hand, the priest shall put some on the tip of the right ear of him who is to be cleansed, on the thumb of his right hand, and on the big toe of his right foot, on the blood of the trespass offering.

The rest of the oil that is in the priest's hand he shall put on the head of him who is to be cleansed. So the priest shall make atonement for him before the Lord.

Leviticus 14:14-18

Think about the significance of this. If everything that was made here and happened here on earth in the physical realm was a copy of the places and procedures in the heavenlies, then all the instructions were some type of foreshadowing.

The scripture tells us that Jesus went into the Holy of Holies to put His blood on the mercy seat. This was not the mercy seat made with hands, which was a mere copy of the original. To be cleansed, the blood had to be applied on the ear to cover what we hear. The blood was put on the thumb to cover what we do. The blood on the toe represented where we go. The blood of Jesus cleansed us from all unrighteousness. The priest also used oil. It represented the Holy Spirit. Once we have been cleansed by the blood of the Lamb, we have the oil applied to everything we hear, everything we put our hands to do and everywhere we walk. But, to top it all off, the anointing oil is poured spiritually over our heads until we are filled to overflowing with the Spirit of God.

Once we fully understand the spiritual implications of the blood, we can begin to access the power that His shed blood bought for us.

blood on
Ear - cover what we hear
Thumb - " " " do
Toe - " where we go
oil - Holy spirit

Chapter 4
Accessing the Power of the Blood

There are so many things that will do us good only if we know how to access them. For example, you can have a key to an automobile. Probably everyone reading this knows how an automobile functions. However, if you took an automobile and put it in the middle of a remote tribe in a jungle that has been untouched by civilization, chances are the people there would lack the knowledge and experience to access the power within the car.

We are so familiar with automobiles, we don't think about how much there is to know about them. We know the key unlocks the door. But that only gets you inside. Once you get inside, you already know where to put the key in the ignition. And you know if you turn the key a certain way, the engine starts. But that is only the beginning. There are rules and regulations for driving a car. That car will do a number of different things for you if you know what to do. It will go backwards. It will go forward. It will turn to the left and the right. It will stop when you push the brake. But your ability to access the power that's under the hood of that car is limited to your knowledge and application.

It's the same way with the Word of God. There's power in the blood of Jesus. Without the knowledge about the blood of Jesus we will never know what to do.

However, even if we study and acquire the knowledge about the blood, it still will not profit us until we act on the knowledge. Knowing what the key will do for an automobile is not enough. You must put action with your knowledge. You must physically get into the car and act on the knowledge. We must do the same thing with the blood. Knowledge without action is like faith without works. It's dead.

> **Thus also faith by itself, if it does not have works, is dead.**
>
> **James 2:17**

In order to access the power of the blood, there are several things a believer needs to know and act upon. First of all, we must realize that everything the blood is supposed to do has already been done in the spirit realm. The first three chapters of this book outline scripture by scripture what Jesus' blood bought for us on the cross. The only thing left for us to do is to have faith in what the blood has done and act on that faith.

To access the blood for salvation, you must:

(1) Believe that Jesus is the Son of God.

(2) Believe that He died on the cross for your sins.

(3) Believe that God raised Him from the dead by His glory and by the Holy Spirit.

The Power is Available Now

Maybe you have already accessed that power and are born again. Then you have experienced this supernatural spiritual change. The old man died. The new man was resurrected to a new life.

But, if you have a cousin or a brother-in-law who's lost, the access to salvation is still available to them. Nothing new or additional has to happen in the spirit realm. What Jesus did for you, He doesn't have to do again for them, because He did it once and for all, for all mankind. The scripture tells us in Acts chapter 2 that we can receive the Spirit of God through a second infilling. We receive the Holy Spirit in the same way we received salvation. We must believe the Holy Spirit is here for us in order to be filled but nothing new has to take place in the spirit realm for us to access that power.

If someone says he doesn't want to operate in the gifts of the Spirit, He will not access the power even though it is available to him. Many places in the Word of God we find it clearly stated that what we believe is what we receive. If you believe what the Word of God says concerning the things that God has already done, then you receive the things God has made available to every believer. There is untold power available to those who believe. It is not enough to know the power exists. We must know how to apply the power in our lives.

When we become Christians, our lives should be changed in such a way that the world will see our good works and be drawn to our heavenly Father. Jesus said to let our lives shine before men.

> **Let your light so shine before men, that they may see your good works and glorify your Father in heaven.**
>
> **Matthew 5:16**

To put it another way, we are to let our light shine in such a way that when other people see the light, they know it's really the power of God embedded within us. They should recognize it to the point that they look to the Source of the power and glorify the God Who put the power in us. If God has provided this great power, should we ignore it out of ignorance or tradition just because we don't understand it?

Living Beyond Our Understanding

There are a lot of things we don't understand that we get ourselves involved in. How many people understood what marriage was about when they first got married? It is doubtful that single people really understand the full impact of what they have just committed themselves to on their wedding day. They are taking a step of faith. You might say a leap of faith.

When people get saved, they know very little about what has happened. They just knew something was missing in their life and what they learned about Jesus made them understand He was the missing part. After they accept Jesus as their Lord and Savior, they start to work out their salvation.

> **Therefore, my beloved, as you have always obeyed, not as in my presence only, but now much more in my absence, work out your own salvation with fear and trembling.**
>
> **Philippians 2:12**

Well, it's the same way with the blood. There is just no way we can completely understand everything there is to understand about the blood of Jesus. We can't stand back and say, "Okay, when I understand everything there is to know about Jesus' blood, I'm going to apply the blood of Jesus to my life. But until then I'm going to study diligently."

We must study and understand all we can, but we cannot limit the power of God to what we understand.

We Access Power by Faith

We must access the power of the blood of Jesus by faith. The Word of God tells us how we can access grace by faith. Romans 5:1,2 says:

Therefore, having been justified by faith, we have peace [Shalom] **with God through our Lord Jesus Christ,**

through whom also we have access by faith into this grace in which we stand.

Romans 5:1-2

We have access to this power of God called grace by faith. Grace is God's willingness to let us use His ability to do what we can't do on our own. If you have something that plagues you, God will step in and do what needs to be done through you. If you could do it on your own, you wouldn't need God. But God is willing to allow you access to His power for everything you need to do.

The greatest scripture on grace is, *"I can do all things through Christ who strengthens me"* (Philippians 4:13). To paraphrase that scripture, it would be like saying, "I can do all things that God wants me to do through Christ who strengthens me to be able to do the things that I couldn't do on my own." If I could do it on my own, I wouldn't need grace. Do you see the power in this statement?

We access this power called grace by faith. That means you not only know the power of grace exists, but you access it by applying faith to it. You must believe that God can do things through you that you formerly didn't believe could be done. You must believe grace is for you. You start by believing God will do what He said He would do. As you believe it, soon everything you say and do will be based on that belief. That's how you access grace.

Another power in the spirit realm we must understand and access is the covenant blood of Jesus. As you learn about the blood and begin to act on all you know, then you must trust God enough to act on what you don't completely understand.

For example, I know all I need to know about electricity. I know that when I turn on the switch in a room, the light goes on or the light goes off, depending on which way I turn the switch. However, I don't have a clue about what makes the electricity run through the wires in the wall. I know how it works, but I don't understand why it works. Just because I don't understand it doesn't mean I don't use it. When I walk into a room and it's dark, it would be foolish for me to get into an extended discussion or argument about the attributes of electricity. I just need light in the room. So, even though I don't fully understand everything there is to know about electricity, I flip the switch anyway, by faith, and then I walk in the light.

If it's in the Word, believe it by faith. Once you can do that, you will find that the blood will start doing things in your life just like it did in the lives of the people in the Bible. When you start seeing what the blood did for the people in the Bible, it will bless your socks off. And the first time you see it work for you, it will change your thinking.

The Word is Saturated with the Blood

Have you ever gone to a car dealership and spotted a new car you liked? You think it's special and unique because it's not like anything you've ever seen before. But when you drive out of the dealership, all of a sudden you begin to notice there are cars like it everywhere. Once you become aware and your eyes are opened, it becomes obvious what you had previously overlooked.

That's the way it is with the Word of God. As you study about the blood, you may not think the blood has too much prominence in the Word of God. But once you start seeing it, you'll find the blood is throughout the scriptures.

There are three things we must review and establish before we dig deeper into the mysteries of the blood.

(1) **Life is in the blood.** Now, if life is in the blood, then death must be in the absence of the blood. "For the life of the flesh is in the blood..." (Leviticus 17:11).

(2) **Everlasting life is in the blood of Jesus.** Jesus said, *"Whoever eats My flesh and drinks My blood has eternal life, and I will raise him up at the last day"* (John 6:54). Jesus is not talking about His physical flesh and blood. This scripture has a spiritual connotation. We commemorate the blood of Jesus by acknowledging His blood when we take communion.

(3) **We access the blood of Jesus by faith.** In the Old Testament, the priest would sacrifice animals to cover sin. Those who came to be cleansed saw the blood. It didn't take faith to know the blood was there. It took faith to know what the blood did. Hebrews 9:12 tells us Jesus entered into the Holy of Holies in heaven and put His blood on the mercy seat once and for all to pay the price for our sin. We receive the blood of Jesus by faith without seeing it.

The Protective Power of the Blood

Romans 5:8,9 says, *"But God demonstrates His own love toward us, in that while we were still sinners, Christ died for us. Much more then, having now been justified by His blood, we shall be saved from wrath through Him."*

We need to realize we are saved from destruction because of the blood of Jesus. It's not your good works that save you from destruction. There are Christians having disasters happen to them all the time. However, the protective power is available for a Christian just by accessing the blood of Jesus that has already been shed.

Let me show you how the blood of the lamb protected the Hebrews before Jesus came to earth. It is found in Exodus 12:21.

> **Then Moses called for all the elders of Israel and said to them, "Pick out and take lambs for yourselves according to your families, and kill the Passover lamb.**
>
> **"And you shall take a bunch of hyssop, dip it in the blood that is in the basin, and strike the lintel and the two doorposts with the blood that is in the basin. And none of you shall go out of the door of his house until morning.**
>
> **"For the Lord will pass through to strike the Egyptians; and when He sees the blood on the lintel and on the two doorposts, the Lord will pass over the door and not allow the destroyer to come into your houses to strike you."**
>
> **Exodus 12:21-23**

That was the protective power of the lamb. Everything that happened in the Old Testament was a foreshadow of what was to come for us under the new covenant.

> **"And you shall observe this thing as an ordinance for you and your sons forever."**
>
> **Exodus 12:24**

The God-fearing Jews of today still observe the Passover. They commemorate the Passover because the death angel passed over their ancestors.

Protection Today

Would you like to have the destroyer stay outside the walls of your home? The blood of Jesus protects the Christian today. Jesus said He didn't come to destroy the law, but to fulfill it.

Do not think that I came to destroy the Law or the Prophets. I did not come to destroy but to fulfill.

Matthew 5:17

God has not changed.

For I am the LORD, I do not change; Therefore you are not consumed, O sons of Jacob.

Malachi 3:6

Jesus has not changed.

Jesus Christ is the same yesterday, today, and forever.

Hebrews 13:8

The same things He did then, He does now. It's just better now because we have a new and better covenant.

But now He has obtained a more excellent ministry, inasmuch as He is also Mediator of a better covenant, which was established on better promises.

For if that first covenant had been faultless, then no place would have been sought for a second.

Hebrews 8:6,7

And for this reason He [Jesus] is the Mediator of the new covenant, by means of death, for the redemption of the transgressions under the first covenant, that those who are called may receive the promise of the eternal inheritance.

Hebrews 9:15

The Israelites had the blood of bulls and goats that covered their sin for a short period of time. But as believers, we have the blood of Jesus that eradicates our sin once and for all.

The Word of Our Testimony

So the great dragon was cast out, that serpent of old, called the Devil and Satan, who deceives the whole world; he was cast to the earth, and his angels were cast out with him.

> **Then I heard a loud voice saying in heaven, "Now salvation, and strength, and the kingdom of our God, and the power of His Christ have come, for the accuser of our brethren, who accused them before our God day and night, has been cast down."**
>
> **Revelation 12:9,10**

Notice that this scripture uses the past tense – the devil *"has been cast down."*

> **And they overcame him by the blood of the Lamb and by the word of their testimony, and they did not love their lives to the death.**
>
> **Revelation 12:11**

We overcome the devil, also known as Satan, by the blood of the Lamb and by the word of our testimony.

This scripture tells me that the word of our testimony is not the blood of the Lamb. There is a difference between the Word of God, our testimony, and the blood.

We access the protective power of the blood by doing the same thing they did in the Old Testament. We apply it. But under the new covenant, we apply it with the words of our mouths. The scripture says, *"Death and life are in the power of the tongue..."* (Proverbs 18:21). That means your life and your death are in the power of your tongue! We must be careful that our words line up with the Word of God. We access the throne of God with our words. What is prayer? Prayer is our words accessing the throne of God.

Remember when the children of Israel were rebelling against Moses? They rebelled with the words of their mouths. Every destruction they brought upon themselves was through their murmuring and complaining. There are examples all through the Word of God to show us that words are powerful. Your word is the way you access the spirit realm. Your words are the way you apply the blood. You speak it. Out of the abundance of the heart, the mouth speaks (Matthew 12:34; Luke 6:45). You will either speak life or death. What is in your heart? It should be an absolute belief in the knowledge that the blood of Jesus will protect you. With that knowledge, you place the blood on the doorposts of your heart, your house and your family. It will protect you and all your household.

The Scarlet Cord

Again, once you understand the blood covenant, you will see it throughout the Word of God. There is an excellent example in Joshua chapter 2.

> **Now Joshua the son of Nun sent out two men from Acacia Grove to spy secretly, saying, "Go, view the land, especially Jericho." So they went, and came to the house of a harlot named Rahab, and lodged there.**
>
> **And it was told the king of Jericho, saying, "Behold, men have come here tonight from the children of Israel to search out the country."**
>
> **So the king of Jericho sent to Rahab, saying, "Bring out the men who have come to you, who have entered your house, for they have come to search out all the country."**
>
> **Then the woman took the two men and hid them...**
>
> **Joshua 2:1-4**

Remember, the people of Jericho were in terror because they knew what God had done for the Hebrews already. The scripture tells us that Rahab had also heard and believed in her heart that God had given the land to the Israelites. Starting in verse 10, she said:

> **"For we have heard how the Lord dried up the water of the Red Sea for you when you came out of Egypt, and what you did to the two kings of the Amor-**

ites who were on the other side of Jordan, Sihon and Og whom you utterly destroyed.

"And as soon as we heard these things, our hearts melted; neither did there remain any more courage in anyone because of you, for the Lord your God, He is God in heaven above and on earth beneath.

"Now therefore, I beg you, swear to me by the Lord, since I have shown you kindness, that you also will show kindness to my father's house, and give me a true token,

"and spare my father, my mother, my brothers, my sisters, and all that they have, and deliver our lives from death."

Joshua 2:10-13

So the men said to her: "We will be blameless of this oath of yours which you have made us swear,

"unless, when we come into the land, you bind this line of scarlet cord in the window through which you let us down, and unless you bring your father, your mother, your brothers, and all your father's household to your own home.

"So it shall be that whoever goes outside the doors of your house into the street, his blood shall be on his own head, and we will be guiltless. And whoever is with you in the house, his blood shall be on our head if a hand if a laid on him."

Then she said, "According to your words, so be it." And she sent them away, and they departed. And she bound the scarlet cord in the window.

Joshua 2:17-19,21

If you look closely, you will notice several key things that are significant to know about applying the blood of the covenant.

In verse 11, Rahab acknowledged that God was God. Because of this, she told the spies she wanted to make a covenant with them concerning her household. The Hebrews understood covenant, but there wasn't time to sacrifice a lamb, so they took a scarlet cord, which represented the blood of the lamb, and told Rahab to put it in the window.

In chapter 6, we read the conclusion of the story, beginning with verse 17:

> **Now the city shall be doomed by the Lord to destruction, it and all who are in it. Only Rahab the harlot shall live, she and all who are with her in the house, because she hid the messengers that we sent.**
>
> **And Joshua spared Rahab the harlot, her father's household, and all that she had....**
>
> **Joshua 6:17,25**

When the two spies came back with the army to utterly destroy the city of Jericho, they were looking for the scarlet cord in the window. Therefore, death passed over Rahab and all of her household. Rahab had faith in the covenant and acted upon it by putting the scarlet cord in the window. Therefore, she, and all who were with her, lived.

There were certain requirements her family had to fulfill before they were saved. First, they had to believe Rahab; and second, they had to act on their belief, or the scripture said they would die (Joshua 2:19). Those in the family were saved because they believed. Look also in Joshua 6:25. The scripture says the covenant not only protected her and her family but, " *...and all that she had....*"

Do you see what this says? God is not only interested in sparing our lives, but by the blood, it says our possessions are included also! When you leave town, you can apply the blood covenant of Jesus as protection over your household. You *can* plead the blood of Jesus! Don't listen to the words of doubt and skepticism. Satan is a liar. There is a real bloodline you can place around your home that Satan has no authority to cross. This isn't just an Old Testament story. In Hebrews 11:31, it says:

> **By faith the harlot Rahab did not perish with those who did not believe, when she had received the spies with peace.**
>
> **Hebrews 11:31**

Did you catch that? By faith she didn't perish with those who did not have faith. The ones who believed God would protect them by a promised covenant did not perish like those who did not believe. Do you see how important faith is?

The Blood Will Make You Complete

The blood not only protects us, it is through the blood that God gives us the ability to do His will.

> **Now may the God of peace who brought up our Lord Jesus from the dead, that great Shepherd of the sheep, through the blood of the everlasting covenant,**
>
> **make you complete in every good work to do His will...**
>
> **Hebrews 13:20,21**

In the New Testament, the apostle Paul sometimes uses sentences that seem like they're a page long. Do you know what I'm saying? But, if you take out all the descriptive phrases and get down to the meat of the verse, Hebrews 13:20,21 says, "May God, through the blood, make you complete to do His will." Let's look at this again.

"May God, through the blood, make you complete to do His will." The blood of Jesus will make you complete so you can do what God wants done. It's so simple, it takes a preacher to confuse it.

His will is that we simply have faith in all He has done with His blood. His blood cleanses, heals, protects and allows us to overcome the trials of life. But we must apply our faith in the blood in order for that to happen. Remember, faith is the catalyst.

Jesus has already applied the blood to the mercy seat in heaven.

> **Not with the blood of goats and calves, but with His own blood He entered the Most Holy Place once for all, having obtained eternal redemption.**
>
> **Hebrews 9:12**

> **For Christ has not entered the holy places made with hands, which are copies of the true, but into heaven itself, now to appear in the presence of God for us.**
>
> **Hebrews 9:24**

Jesus is in heaven as our advocate. He is there with God on our behalf. The blood is in heaven on the mercy seat. We must acknowledge the power of the blood and what the blood has done by faith. When we do that, we will be protected.

Psalm 9:12 says, *"When He avenges blood, He remembers them; He does not forget the cry of the humble."*

The word *"cry"* can also mean "pleading." We must plead our case. Our witness is the blood. Our case is based upon the blood evidence. Because of the evidence of the blood presented in the courtroom of heaven, we win. We win!

When the judge says, "How do you plead?" you say, "I plead the blood of Jesus!" The evidence proves beyond any doubt that light overpowers darkness and that God is victorious in heaven and earth. The evidence is the blood of Jesus.

Chapter 5
Understanding the New Covenant

There are some practical aspects we need to be aware of if we want to access the covenant of God. There are things in the Word of God that show us how the new covenant differs from the old covenant.

In the Old Testament the Israelites understood that killing an animal and applying the blood was the way God ratified covenants.

But in the New Testament, we are under a different set of rules. Hebrews 8:6 says it is a better covenant. That doesn't mean the Old Testament is gone because Jesus didn't come to destroy the Old Testament law. He came to fulfill it (Matthew 5:17). Through fulfilling it, He redeemed us from the curse of it.

A Covenant is a Legal Document

Any time you enter into a contract, for example, the selling of a house, both the buyer and the seller sign the contract. The contract is not binding and valid until both parties involved have signed and completed the transaction.

It's the same way concerning the promises of the new covenant. God has already ratified the contract with the blood of Jesus. The only ones left to sign the contract are those who choose to believe and accept the offer of salvation.

The Word of God doesn't say we must use the blood of bulls or goats under the new covenant. The way we ratify our part of the covenant is with the words of our mouth. Romans 10:9 says, *"...If you confess with your mouth the Lord Jesus and believe in your heart that God has raised Him from the dead, you will be saved."*

Jesus has already signed His portion of your contract with His blood, but you have to sign your portion with your words for it to be valid.

The Importance of Our Words

The Word of God has countless scriptures to show us that we will have what we speak. Our words are vitally important. Remember, life and death are in the power of the tongue (Proverbs 18:21). The reason Jesus warned us about using idle or useless words in Matthew 12:36 was because our words have the power to accept or reject the promises found in our covenant with God. What we confess is a very important thing. Sometimes we forget how important our words actually are. In Ecclesiastes 5:2,3 it says, *"Do not be rash with your mouth, And let not your heart utter anything hastily before God. For God is in heaven, and you on earth; therefore let your words be few. For a dream comes through much activity, And a fool's voice is known by his many words."*

Have you ever met somebody that had a lot of words? If your words are few, you will probably have more time to think. We must understand that words are important.

Using Words to Overcome

Revelation 12:11 says, *"And they overcame him by the blood of the Lamb, and by the word of their testimony."*

Your blood cannot save you. Your blood cannot heal you. Your blood cannot protect you. But the blood of Jesus can do it all. Jesus shed His blood so you could have overcoming power. Do you need to overcome something in your life? Well, you have overcoming power by the blood of the Lamb and by the word of your testimony.

Proverbs 10:11 says, *"The mouth of the righteous is a well of life..."*

The Bible tells us that out of the abundance of the heart the mouth speaks, but it's your mind that determines what you put into your heart. In other words, you can dip down into that well and draw out life. God gave you a brain to think with. Your brain, which determines what you put into your heart, controls your mouth.

The Words We Hear are the Words We Speak

If we are serious about our Christian walk, sometimes we need to be wise enough to say, "I don't choose to hear that." I respect my wife, Loretta, because she's not afraid to take a stand in this area. We have decided we will not allow unwholesome TV shows or movies in our home. Why? If we watch them, we're allowing our eyes and ears to bring unhealthy thoughts into our minds. Whatever comes into our minds will be what we meditate on and those things will eventually enter our hearts. And, out of the abundance of the heart, the mouth will speak.

A little girl about three years old was in my office with her grandmother. Somebody walked in the office and asked her what she was doing. The little girl said, "Coloring. I love to color." The two talked for a minute and the adult asked, "Can I have your book?" The person was teasing the little girl. The little girl replied, "Get your [blank] hands off my book."

This little girl was young enough that she didn't understand how to govern what had come into her mind and lodged in her heart. This is why we need to protect our children. They don't know what they should have or shouldn't have in their hearts.

This incident proved to be a true illustration of Matthew 12:34, because out of the abundance of her heart, her mouth spoke. Your kids pick up what you're speaking, and what you say will come out of their mouths. The fact is it doesn't change when we get to be adults. The same principle works regardless of who we are or how much we don't think it applies to us. Out of the abundance of the heart, the mouth speaks. It is a spiritual principle.

God's Plan is Simple

In Proverbs 4:20 where the scripture begins, *"My son,"* it is talking to us. As born-again believers, we are children of the King. We are born into the kingdom. We are inheritors of the promise. Every biblical promise and all the Word of God applies to us if we confess with our mouths and accept the promises. Now, how do we sign the contract on our side of the promise? We either receive it and confess that we receive it, or we reject it and confess that we reject it. It's all done with our words.

This is one thing about the Word of God we need to understand as Christians. It's God's plan. We can kick as much as we want to, but the only thing that is going to work is when we follow His plan. Our words are important because that's how God planned it.

If you think that's too simple, maybe you need to realize that God tried to make it as simple as He could for us. Have you ever thought that God loved us so much that He didn't want to make His plans difficult? He didn't say that in order to be saved you have to walk one thousand miles, or pray twenty-two days, or fast for a month. His plan only requires that you believe in your heart and confess with your mouth that Jesus Christ is Lord. And when you confess that, you've signed your half of the contract and it becomes valid. You've got eternal life. It's so simple and yet some people will still miss it.

Giving Our Attention to His Word

Proverbs 4:20 says, *"My son, give attention to my words..."* God is carefully telling us to pay attention, take in, meditate on and surround ourselves with His words.

Why is He directing us? Because He knows if we pay close attention to what He is saying, that out of the abundance of our hearts our mouths will speak the right things.

When you get yourself into a jam or you're backed up against the wall, you don't have time to think about what God's Word says. It's like the little girl in my office with the coloring book. She didn't think about it. She didn't ponder her response. She simply thought this adult was trying to take her coloring book and so what was in her heart just came out of her mouth.

You may be driving down the highway and a drunk driver swerves into your lane and there appears to be no way of escape. What you don't need to say at that moment is, "Oh, my gosh, I'm going to die!" If you've got the Word of God in your heart, you will probably end up saying something like, "Jesus!!!" The result will be 180-degrees different because the Word of God says you get what you speak. So if we keep the Word of God in our hearts, it will be in our mouths at the times we need it, even when it's needed quickly in a moment of crisis. Then we will be protected.

Proverbs 4:20 says, *"My son, give attention to my words; incline your ear to my sayings."*

Loretta and I were on an airplane the other day and a lady near us read a book the entire trip. You could tell by the cover of the book that it wasn't a survey on the Book of John. The picture on the front cover indicated the book was about lust and intrigue. If we dwell on subjects the world has to offer like adultery, fornication and big business deals where people are trying to rip you off, that's what you're going to have in your heart. It will also be what's going to come out of your mouth. Personally, what I want to come out of my mouth is something that's going to help me.

Getting Proverbs 4:20 down in your heart can change your life. It can take you from living a life of defeat into living a life of victory. *"My son, give attention to my words; incline your ear to my sayings."*

When you get into the Word of God, you will start hungering for more Word and your faith will increase.

> **So then faith comes by hearing, and hearing by the word of God.**
>
> **Romans 10:17**

Likewise, if you allow the devil to lure your flesh into the things of the world, you will not be satisfied with just a little bit. Sin is progressive.

Our Words Progress into Actions

I got a letter some time ago from a prisoner who was in the cell next to a nationally known rapist and serial killer. We had sent some Bibles through our prison ministry, *Bibles Behind Bars,* and he had received one through the prison chaplain. He told us the Bible he received from us was the only thing he had not stolen or gotten through some illegal means. It's amazing there are still people in the United States who don't have a Bible!

In his letter he made reference to the serial killer in the cell next to him. Later in the week there was a news documentary about this particular serial killer. In the documentary they revealed some interesting details that were confirmed to me in this letter. The strongest point was this: sin is progressive. The serial killer didn't wake up one day and decide to start murdering women. It was said that he started out looking at newsstand pornographic literature. After a while that wasn't enough to satisfy his lust. It just got worse and worse. A lot of people don't realize that the things of the devil are progressive, just like the things of God are progressive.

It's the same way with our words. We can become so used to hearing things that are bad that we no longer think they're bad anymore. The Bible says in 1 Timothy 4:2 our consciences become seared because we hear something that's wrong for so long that we don't realize it's wrong anymore. In fact, we think it's right.

Proverbs 4:20 says to pay attention to His words. In verse 21 it says:

> **Let them not depart from your sight; keep them in the center of your heart.**
>
> **For they are life to those who find them, healing and health to all their flesh.**
>
> **Proverbs 4:21,22 (AMP)**

The word health in this verse can also be translated "medicine" or "strength." When we take the Word of God into our minds, it enters our hearts. The Word becomes so alive that it moves from the spiritual realm into the physical realm and heals our flesh. According to the Word of God, what starts out as a spiritual thing can result in medicine and strength to our flesh!

This spiritual law was manifested in our church when the doctors told one of our members that his situation was terminal. They were not giving him any hope. But, Ed, and his wife, Linda, had a lot of hope. Do you know what the devil wanted out of Ed and Linda? He wanted their words. That's what God wanted too. God wanted them to overcome the devil by the blood of the Lamb and by the word of their testimony. God wanted them to say what He said about their situation. Life, according to the Word of God, is when we incline our ears and eyes to the Word of God and we put the Word of God in our hearts. Ed is alive and well today because he would not let the devil steal his confession.

> **...Whoever says to this mountain, "Be removed and be cast into the sea," and does not doubt in his heart, but believes that those things he says will be done, he will have whatever he says.**
>
> **Mark 11:23**

Now, three times in this one verse Jesus talked about what you "say." Why didn't Jesus say, "If you've got a problem in your life, just believe God and it will go away?" Because God's plan says you've got to believe in your heart and confess it with your mouth.

Again, Revelation 12:11 says, *"And they overcame him by the blood of the Lamb"* — one half of the contract — *"and by the word of their testimony"* — the other half of the contract. It's not enough to just think it's going to be okay. What matters to God is if you believe it in your heart and confess it with your mouth. The reason it matters to God is because it is a spiritual law that cannot be waived or overturned. He wants abundant life for His children.

How to Stop Doubting God

The scripture tells us in Romans 10:17, *"So then faith comes by hearing, and hearing by the word of God."* The principle is this: What you hear goes into your mind. If you mediate and dwell on it, it goes into your heart. Then from your heart, it goes to your mouth. When you speak your heart, you hear your heart. If the Word is what is in your heart, the result is increased faith because you hear the Word. The fact that it is your mouth speaking what you hear is irrelevant. The Word produces faith regardless of the mouth speaking it.

How do you get rid of the doubt that is already lodged in your heart from years of unbelief? Doubt leaves when the Word becomes a way of life. In with the Word — out with the doubt.

The only way you're going to have depth of belief and great faith is to confess God's Word all the time.

> **This Book of the Law shall not depart from your mouth, but you shall meditate in it day and night, that you may observe to do according to all that is written in it. For then you will make your way prosperous, and then you will have good success.**
>
> **Joshua 1:8**

If you want to be able to tell your mountains — "be removed and be cast into the sea" — confessing the Word will have to become your lifestyle.

That's why I get up in the morning and plead the blood of Jesus over my household. I thank God that my household is delivered. I thank God that my children are going to be safe throughout the day. I thank God that His Word rules supreme in my house. I do this on a daily basis, and you can too. Don't wait until you have a crisis to start pleading the blood and speaking the Word.

One of my favorite illustrations involves a puny little guy who meets the big, muscle-bound man in the alley at midnight. "Give me your money!" says the big bully. At this point, the puny little guy doesn't have time to go home, join a health club, work out, build up his muscles, come back and fight the bully. The bully is not going to let him do that! Waiting to prepare until the day of the fight is foolishness and laughable.

However, many Christians live their spiritual lives that way. They wait until the devil (the bully) meets them in the ally at midnight (an unexpected time and place) and they attempt to fast, pray, read the Word, build up their faith and plead the blood in order to keep from being destroyed. The problem is, they are not doing it in faith. They are doing it in desperation as a result of fear from the attack. A great man of God preached a sermon called "You Can't Teach a Drowning Man to Swim." God's plan is for us to daily renew our minds and to daily build our faith through the Word and to daily plead the blood of Jesus for our protection. Waiting until there is a crisis is foolish.

Vitamin "W"

We need to take in the Word of God on a daily basis. When the devil jumps in our path and gets nose to nose with us, we can say, "Move out of my way, Satan. There's no place for you here. Be gone in the name of Jesus. I do not accept this disaster in my life. I don't accept it, because God is my Deliverer."

But if you don't have the Word of God constantly in your heart, when the devil jumps in your path, you may say, "Get out of my path," but deep down inside you're saying, "I know you won't. It works for my pastor, but it's not going to work for me."

It will work for you if you've been exercising in the Word on a daily basis. The time to start is now because the promises of God are for you!

Chapter 6

How to Gain Access to the Promises of God

Hopefully, at this point, your knowledge about the blood covenant has grown. Now you need to know how to put this power to work so it can impact your life and change the things you need changed around you. The blood of Jesus can change your life. The Word of God brings life to your flesh.

> **My son, give attention to my words; incline your ear to my sayings.**
>
> **Do not let them** [His words] **depart from your eyes; keep them** [His words] **in the midst of your heart;**
>
> **For they are life to those who find them, and health** [which means medicine or strength] **to all their flesh**
>
> **Proverbs 4:20-22**

If we can take the Word of God and move it from our minds into our hearts, it not only moves things in the spirit realm, but it will manifest things in the physical realm also. God's Word is life to your spirit, and according to His Word, it can also be life to all your flesh.

Remember, the scripture that tells us the way to overcome is in Revelation 12:11: *"And they overcame him* [the devil] *by the blood of the Lamb, and by the word of their testimony."* God wants your words to be a repeat of what

He says. He knows if your words are a repeat of what He says, then you will be able to live and enjoy the promises He wants to give you with those words.

But, the devil wants you to repeat what he says. John 8:44 says Satan is a liar and the father of lies. He will try to get you to say what he wants. He's smart enough to know that what you say is what you will eventually believe. The devil knows you will get what you say because that is the way God planned it. God wants the best for you. He wants you to speak the promises that are built upon the blood covenant. When you speak those promises, you access the abundant life God planned for you to enjoy.

God's Abundant Covenant

There's a difference between the promises of God and the covenant of God. Some people think the promises are the covenant. Actually, the promises are built on the covenant. When you sign the covenant with your words, you become a born-again believer. That means you have the foundation to access all the promises of God. The promises are not automatic. You can ratify the covenant and still not enjoy all the promises. The promises found in the Word include health, prosperity, proper relationships and every other good thing. But we don't start out with all these promises working in our lives even though we're born-again believers. Why? Because God planned for us to access them as we believe in the Word. It's up to each Christian to take the steps of applying God's Word so it will take root in his heart.

How to Become Word Minded

We must be word-minded and not sense-minded. Here's how the devil works against us. He wants us to start thinking about his words. The devil says things like, "Just a little bit of a misnumbering on your tax return is okay." The devil says, "It's okay to drive 70 in a 65-mile-an-hour zone." He starts with little things. (Luke 16:10). A convicted rapist and murderer didn't wake up one day as a serial killer. He started by reading soft pornography. But after a while, that didn't take care of his thirst. So he went to a little harder core porn, and then when that no longer satisfied, he began to act out his fantasies. The things of the devil are progressive.

The things of God are also progressive. Once you taste the Word of God, you find your hunger and thirst grows for His Word. You just want more and more and more.

The Battle for Your Thoughts

The battlefield of faith is found in our minds. We need to keep our minds filled with the things of God. That's why the Bible tells you what to do when you have a thought that's not right. Second Corinthians 10:4,5 says you reject it, you cast it down and you get rid of it so it doesn't trickle down into your heart. Once it gets into your heart, out of the abundance of the heart you'll start speaking it. And, what you say is what you get.

Let's look again at Mark 11:23. Jesus is speaking and He says, *"...Whoever says to that mountain, 'Be removed and be cast into the sea,' and does not doubt in his heart, but believes that those things he says will be done, he will have whatever he says."*

Again, in this one verse, Jesus talks about what you say three times. He knew He needed to emphasize this spiritual principle about entering the spirit realm through words for us to understand it.

You get your prayer to the throne of God by speaking it. There's no place in the Word of God where it talks about silent prayer. Does that surprise you? God wants us to speak our prayers. Jesus spoke to God.

> **Then they took away the stone from the place where the dead man was lying. And Jesus lifted up His eyes and said, "Father, I thank You that You have heard Me."**
>
> **John 11:41**

> **Jesus spoke these words, lifted up His eyes to heaven, and said: "Father, the hour has come. Glorify Your Son, that Your Son also may glorify You."**
>
> **John 17:1**

We get what we say. There is a great battle taking place over your thought life because nothing happens in the spirit realm until what you think drops down into your heart. For out of the abundance of the heart, the mouth speaks.

Agreeing with the Word of God

Do you want victory in the spirit realm? You've got to speak it. As a minister of the gospel, my responsibility is to repeat what God says — not to make up my own theories. I didn't make up the rules. I must do what He says to do. I must say what He says to say. His Word is His will. Look at the confidence God allows us to have in what we say when we speak His Word. 1 John 5:14 says, *"Now this is the confidence that we have in Him, that if we ask anything according to His will, He hears us."*

We must be word-minded people. Word-minded people are steady because the Word of God is steady. Sense-minded people are ruled by how they feel as perceived by the five senses — what they taste, touch, hear, smell and see. Sense-minded people are up and down.

I call them "roller coaster" or "yo-yo" Christians because they are driven by their senses. If the Word of God is what you believe, you'll be steady because the Word of God doesn't vary. God doesn't say that one day He'll bless you and the next day He'll curse you. The Word of God says it is His will to heal you. Therefore, if you're attacked with sickness in your body, you're going to be steady because you know it's God's will that you be healed, set free and live a wonderful life. You're going to be steady in your mind regardless of how you feel in your body if you are Word-minded.

You Get What You Speak

When people who are driven by their senses, wake up and feel good, they say, "Whoa, this is a good day! Man, I haven't had a day like this in a long time. I sure hope it lasts, because I felt like a mess yesterday."

The next day when they wake up in a mess, they say, "Oh, man, I knew it wouldn't last." Sense-minded people are snared by the words of their mouth (Proverbs 18:7).

It's amazing what some people say. You hear Christian people say things like, "You know, every time I eat at a restaurant I get sick. And I know it's true because I just ate at a restaurant yesterday and I got sick." Did you ever stop to think what they are saying about themselves?

"I'm always afraid when I get on airplanes. Airplanes scare me. I was just on a flight last week and I was scared to death." The Word of God says what they believe is what they speak. They're going to get what they speak. The result is fear and no peace or joy on the flight.

"No one likes me." "My mother always told me I wouldn't amount to anything." "I'd like to hold down a job, but I can't." I could go on with a lot more phrases I hear because that's the way many people think, therefore they speak it. They have thought the same thoughts so long that the thoughts are down into their hearts. And out of the abundance of their hearts, they have spoken it over and over. Their heart becomes so negative and full of doubt that it seems like nothing will ever change.

Since it seems like nothing will ever change, then these sense-minded people believe nothing will ever change. Because they see nothing changing in their life, they believe nothing will ever change, and they continue to speak that nothing will ever change and the result is — nothing changes.

Once I was counseling with a person who was full of doubt and unbelief. He thought he was worthless and his life was a mess and he spoke that he was worthless and his life was beyond repair. After much teaching and explaining to him about how he would get what he spoke, his comment was this, "That may work for some people, but it won't work for me. I've tried to understand God's Word, but I haven't been able to and I don't think I ever will." In the years since this counseling session, I must confess, he was right.

Where the Change Starts

We are a three-part being. We are body, soul and spirit, and we need to understand that what we bring into the area of the soul drops down into our inner man. The Word within our spiritual heart affects our physical heart.

The scripture tells us that there's a difference between revelation knowledge and sense knowledge. Sense knowledge involves the eyes and ears. Revelation knowledge involves the inner man. It's important to understand how critical our words are.

Again, under the new covenant we apply the blood of Jesus with our mouth. We apply the blood of Jesus by confessing what we believe to be true. As we understand the covenant blood, it brings a whole new meaning to Revelation 12:11.

> **And they have overcome (conquered) him by means of the blood of the Lamb and by the utterance of their testimony, for they did not love and cling to life even when faced with death — holding their lives cheap till they had to die [for their witnessing].**
>
> **Revelation 12:11 (AMP)**

It is important for you to have a revelation of this for yourself. Knowing it is one thing, but understanding how to apply the blood is something else. Remember, God wants your words and the devil wants your words. The first time you open your mouth and speak doubt and unbelief concerning a spiritual promise, that portion (promise) of the contract is not valid for you. It does not mean the contract is not valid, but that portion will remain unfulfilled until you ratify it with the correct confession.

The Hebrews were told to march around Jericho for six days and not say a word. The purpose could have been to keep strife, contention, doubt and unbelief from coming out of their mouths, because God knew what was in their hearts. So, if you find yourself standing nose to nose with the devil and you don't know what to say, but you've done all you know to do, stand with your mouth shut!

Our Words are Important

> **Keep your heart with all diligence, for out of it spring the issues of life.**
>
> **Put away from you a deceitful mouth, and put perverse lips far from you.**
>
> **Proverbs 4:23,24**

The issues of life spring out of your heart. But they get out of your heart through your lips, because out of the abundance of the heart the mouth speaks.

Look at what Jesus told his disciples in Matthew 15:16-20:

> **So Jesus said, "Are you also still without understanding?**
>
> **"Do you not yet understand that whatever enters the mouth goes into the stomach and is eliminated?**
>
> **"But those things which proceed out of the mouth come from the heart, and they defile a man.**
>
> **"For out of the heart proceed evil thoughts, murders, adulteries, fornications, thefts, false witness, blasphemies.**
>
> **"These are the things which defile a man, but to eat with unwashed hands does not defile a man."**
>
> **Matthew 15:16-20**

Look closely at what Jesus is saying here. If a person has sin in his heart, it's going to come out through his mouth. And what proceeds out of his mouth is what defiles him. So, to be undefiled we must be sure the abundance of our hearts only brings forth what the Word of God says. We cannot have two confessions. Matthew chapter 12 says:

> **"Either make the tree good and its fruit good, or else make the tree bad and its fruit bad; for a tree is known by its fruit.**
>
> **"Brood of vipers! How can you, being evil, speak good things? For out of the abundance of the heart, the mouth speaks.**
>
> **"A good man out of the good treasure of his heart brings forth good things, and an evil man out of the evil treasure brings forth evil things.**

"But I say to you that every idle word men may speak, they will give account of it in the day of judgment."

Matthew 12:33-36

Our words are important. How can you have a good marriage? You start by using good words. You may say, "Well, actions speak louder than words." Well, let me tell you this. The way to change negative actions must begin with words. You start with good words because the one who says them also hears them. The first thing a person must change is his confession. As long as he keeps confessing it, he is going to continue to hear it. The next thing you know, it gets into his heart. Then, instead of just speaking it out of brain knowledge, he starts speaking it out of heart knowledge. All of a sudden, he starts acting on it. In the beginning, he may not. But, after a while, actions will begin to follow his words. And it all started with the words of his mouth.

The reverse is also true. How does a marriage fall apart? It happens the same way. I've heard men say things like, "My wife's an idiot."

"She doesn't know how to act at parties."

"She's a jerk."

"She doesn't know how to do anything right."

"She's an albatross around my neck."

Maybe they don't believe it at the time, but you know what? After they say it long enough, they start believing it. When it gets into their heart, they'll believe what they're saying and start acting on it.

Your words will develop into actions. Your words can create beliefs. If they line up with the Word of God, they will create faith. If they line up with the words of the devil, they'll create fear, doubt and unbelief. Either way, you get what you speak.

Working the Word

There is a true story of a young man in a railroad station who was watching an elderly gentleman read the signs up on the wall that were in very small print.

The young man was thinking, "How can that man, being as old as he is, read that small print?" Then he noticed that the older gentleman's hair was still a thick, rich black. When the gentleman turned around and smiled, the young observer could tell his teeth were still his own. The young man was so overwhelmed, he finally went up to the man and said, "Sir, can I ask how old are you?" The gentleman said, "I'm 90."

At this, the young observer said, "It's obvious you're in great shape. You haven't lost your hair or your teeth, and you can read signs I can hardly read. Why is this so?"

The gentleman replied, "From an early age I realized that the Word of God said you get what you say. So, I have spoken all my life that my hair is thick and full of color, that my teeth shall not depart far from me" and he named several other confessions. At last, he said, "I confess these things every day. Everybody thought I was an idiot when I was young, but now that I'm getting older they're beginning to realize I wasn't an idiot after all."

Do you see that Jesus told the truth when He said in Mark 11:23 that you can have whatever you say?

A large percentage of the people who will read this book will have ratified the covenant by confessing Jesus as Lord and Savior. But are they getting all of the blessings that are promised to them?

Proverbs 18:21 says, *"Death and life are in the power of the tongue, and those who love it will eat its fruit."* Do you want joy in your life? Proverbs 15:23 says, *"A man has joy by the answer of his mouth..."* The Word of God is telling you your life is determined by what you say. Let every moment be an adventure in your Christian life.

You may be thinking, "Well, it's too late for me." The devil would love to have you believe it's too late. It's never too late to start confessing the Word of God on a daily basis and pleading the blood of Jesus over yourself. The Word will always be life to all your flesh.

I heard another true story that shows us just how much what we believe can be manifested. If it can be manifested in the negative, think of how much more God will do when our hearts are filled with His Word.

An unsaved woman went in to see her doctor because she had a high fever. This happened several times. About the third time the doctor said, "You know, you do have a fever, but I can't find anything wrong with you whatsoever."

After the doctor looked at her a while, he said, "You've been disgusted about two or three different things since you've come in and you keep making the statement, 'That just burns me up.'" The doctor said, "Let's try a little experiment. For the next two weeks, don't say, 'That burns me up.'" This was not a Christian doctor who knew the spiritual principles of the Word of God. But after two weeks, the lady's fever went away.

Spiritual laws work. Like natural laws, they work whether you believe them or not. If you jump off of a building, gravity works whether you believe it will or not. Some people are blessed because they speak God's Word even though they may not understand why they are being blessed. The promises are conditional. The laws are established.

Think of how much more we can enjoy life when we grab hold of the promises in the blood covenant. We were designed to be more than conquerors in this life.

Yet in all these things we are more than conquerors through Him who loved us.

Romans 8:37

We are overcomers. When the destroyer gets to my house, he hits a spiritual shield and he bumps over it, because the blood of the Lamb covers my house.

Don't wait. Start today by making this daily confession.

Say this out loud:

"I believe in the power of the blood of Jesus Christ. I believe His blood was shed for my salvation, redemption, protection and eternal life. Because I believe it and confess it, I apply by faith the blood of Jesus on the doorposts of my heart and my home. I plead the blood of Jesus over me, my spouse, my children, my grandchildren and all that I possess. I draw a blood line around my entire family, our homes and all that is within them. The destroyer must pass over my household. He has no right to enter. I speak the protection of Psalm 91 over my household and I thank God for protecting me."

Chapter 7

The Power to Stand

For years the church has talked about the power of God and the name of Jesus. We've talked about power in the Word of God. We've talked about power in the blood. We've even sung the song, "There is power, power, wonder-working power in the blood...." Everybody agrees there's power. Everybody agrees that the Lord God Almighty sent Jesus to put Satan under His feet. We know we are the body of Christ and the devil is a defeated foe. However, if all that is true, why is it that when the devil comes against us, so many Christians don't know how to access the power to put down the devil?

We must remember that the Word also says we have a better covenant as a New Testament believer. Under the new covenant, we have been given the authority and power, by using the name of Jesus, to rebuke the devourer with our own words. Under the new covenant, we are no longer waiting for God to solve our problem. God is waiting on us to use the power of the blood and the name and the Word that He has already given us.

> **Behold, I give you the authority to trample on serpents and scorpions, and over all the power of the enemy, and nothing shall by any means hurt you.**
>
> **Luke 10:19**

By so much more Jesus has become a surety of a better covenant.

Hebrews 7:22

But as it now is, He [Christ] has acquired a [priestly] ministry which is as much superior and more excellent [than the old] as the covenant — the agreement — of which He is the Mediator (the Arbiter, Agent) is superior and more excellent; [because] it is enacted and rests upon more important (sublimer, higher and nobler) promises.

Hebrews 8:6 (AMP)

America is a Blessed Land

According to a major university study, if we could shrink the earth's population to a village of precisely one hundred people, with all the existing human ratios remaining the same, here's what this town of one hundred would look like at the turn of the millennium.

Fifty-seven would be Asians, twenty-one would be Europeans, fourteen would be from the Western hemisphere and eight would be from Africa. Fifty-two of the one hundred people would be female. Forty-eight would be male. Seventy would be non-Christian. Thirty would claim to be Christian. Eighty-nine would be heterosexual. Eleven would be homosexual.

Six people would possess fifty-nine percent of the entire world's wealth, and all six people would be from the United States of America. Eighty out of a hundred would live in substandard housing. Seventy of the hundred people in this village would be unable to read. Fifty of these hundred people would suffer from malnutrition. One would be near death. One would be near birth. Only one would have a college education. Only one would own a computer.

Anyone reading this has to stop and think how truly blessed those of us living in the United States of

America are. We are part of a unique group. The reason is, we live in a blessed nation. This nation is blessed because the government was founded on the principle of "In God We Trust" and we love Israel.

This nation has more Word taught in it than any place in the world. There are many places in the world today where it is illegal to own a Bible. In some countries you could be executed just for having a Bible in your possession.

In a certain country a group of Christians got together in late 1999 in answer to an advertisement. The ad appeared in a newspaper owned by the state. The ad said, "If you are a Christian and you would like to join us for a Christian meeting, come ..." and the meeting place was named. It was a public place. Several thousand people answered the ad by showing up. Hundreds were executed on the spot. Others were beaten and arrested.

Let's get real. Those of us who live in the United States of America are not facing persecution because we are Christian. Yes, there may be some people you work with who make fun of you because they don't know Jesus as their Savior. But let's look at the reality of this. There are pockets of persecution even in the United States and some of it is severe, but compared to the rest of the world, what most people suffer doesn't even count as persecution. However, just because our persecution in most places in the USA is small, we should never take our freedom for granted.

Stand Up and Use Your Authority

Stand up for who you are! You are a member of the body of Christ. You have abilities and power behind you that the world can't comprehend! The power of God is not adjusted to great power or small power by the location of a Christian. In other words, the power of the blood for protection is just as great in the darkest country of the world as it is in the free world. This is why we were commanded by our Lord to go and teach the good news of the Word to all nations. Without the knowledge of the protective power of the blood, a Christian will not access it. Unless we apply the blood to the doorpost of our homes and hearts, the destroyer will not pass over.

We, as Christians, have the awesome responsibility to tell the world of this power.

> **"My people are destroyed for lack of knowledge."**
>
> **Hosea 4:6**

> **"Go therefore and make disciples of all the nations, baptizing them in the name of the Father and of the Son and of the Holy Spirit,**
>
> **"teaching them to observe all things that I have commanded you; and lo, I am with you always, *even* to the end of the age." Amen.**
>
> **Matthew 28:19,20**

No weapon formed against you can prosper (Isaiah 54:17). There is nothing that can come against you that cannot be conquered by using the words of your mouth!

You have the Word of God, the name and the blood of Jesus available on a moment's notice! You are the only one who is keeping you from using this awesome power!

Again, the devil is a defeated foe. The only authority and power he has is what we give him. So if the devil is coming against you, you can make him stop!

When you get face to face with the devil, don't back off. Just put your finger in his face and say, "Be gone! You have no right here. In the name of Jesus, get out of my path!"

Greater is He That is in You

We have the freedom to study about the blood of Jesus and the ability, if we'll take it, to use the blood of Jesus in our lives totally unhindered by man.

When we go out into the world we can be mighty warriors. We don't have to be beaten down wimps. We don't have to go into the workplace and have people look at us and make fun of us and watch us cower and say, "Well, I'd better not say anything. I sure don't want to embarrass myself." Stand up for who you are! Stand up for who He is. *"Greater is He that is in you than he that is in the world."* (1 John 4:4).

There is a way to activate the power of God and keep the devil out of your face. When he comes against your home, your family or your finances, there is something you can do to push back the devil and keep him out. Now, somebody may say, "Does that mean we can kick the devil off the face of the earth?" No! There are limits to your authority. That is why you must have the knowledge of what God says for you to do.

I was in a Bible study one time when I heard a lady pray, "And, Satan, I command you back to hell from whence you came." The Bible doesn't say the devil has ever been to hell, and he certainly doesn't want to go there anyway. The Bible prophetically tells us when the devil is going to be cast into hell in Revelation 20:10. We must know how God says to handle the devil and we must know what we're doing. The devil may be loose in the spirit realm on the earth, but we can keep him and the forces of the enemy out of our space. Your words are powerful, but your words will never override God's prophecy.

Therefore submit to God. Resist the devil and he will flee from you.

James 4:7

When the Hebrews were getting ready to leave Egypt, the Lord warned them the destroyer would come to kill the firstborn male of every family — unless they took the blood of a lamb and put it on the doorpost (Exodus 12:23). He didn't say the destroyer wouldn't come. God told them how to access the power of the blood so that when the destroyer got to their house, he would pass over it because of the blood.

Sometimes Christians pray that the destroyer won't show up at their house. The destroyer will show up at your house, but with the blood of Jesus applied on the doorpost of your house, the destroyer will pass over. You are not going to cast the devil into hell, but you can keep the devil out of your house and out of your life.

We've already learned that in Old Testament times the Hebrews were required to place the actual blood of a slain lamb over their doorpost. Under the new covenant, we do the same thing; however, instead of using the physical blood of the lamb, we symbolically take the blood that was shed by Jesus two thousand years ago and apply it to our own household with the words of our mouth.

The Word of God tells us we can access the spirit realm with our words. Everything we do in the spirit realm is through our words. When we pray, we speak words to the Father in the name of Jesus. Because we are born-again believers, bought by the blood that Jesus shed, we have access to the Father and His power through our words. If you do not speak to the Father, the Father doesn't hear you. If you don't apply the blood of Jesus with your words, the blood of Jesus will not be applied in that area of your life.

Ask to Receive

In Luke 11:13, the scripture tells us that if our earthly fathers being evil can still give us good gifts, how much more the heavenly Father will give the Holy Spirit to him who asks. So, to receive of the Father in the spirit realm, we ask.

In James 4:2, it says that many of us don't receive because we don't ask. How do you ask? You ask with the words of your mouth.

I have a grandson who is three years old. If he goes, "Ah, ah, ah, ah," and he's pointing toward the catsup or something, we don't give it to him. We treat him the same way God treats His children. We say, "Tell us what you want." He must say it. Eventually we will train him to say, "Would you pass the catsup, please?"

When we first started training our children and they were little, they did not say, "Would you pass the catsup, please?" At first they said, "Catsup, catsup, catsup." Later we taught them to speak more correctly and they would say, "Catsup, please." Then one day they learned to say, "Would you pass the catsup, please?" It was a gradual, progressive improvement of their speech to get them to clearly say what they wanted so we could give it to them because they asked properly.

> **You lust and do not have. You murder and covet and cannot obtain. You fight and war. Yet you do not have because you do not ask.**
>
> **You ask and do not receive, because you ask amiss, that you may spend *it* on your pleasures.**
>
> **James 4:2,3**

James 4:2 clearly says that if you don't ask, you won't receive. Sometimes, we may ask, but we still don't receive because we didn't ask with the right motives. We need to understand how to access the blood of Jesus and apply it by faith in the way God says to ask.

Be Determined to Receive

Right thinking leads to right believing. Right believing leads to right speaking and right speaking leads to right acting. If you determine to do it, you will do it.

I know what it's like to be determined. Loretta and I lived in Kansas City right after we got married and I needed a job badly. I went to a drafting company and the only opening they had was for an engineer to design reinforcing steel for part of Interstate 70 and five public schools. When they asked me if I could do it, I said, "Yes, I can do it." They gave me drafting equipment and my own desk between two civil engineers.

I mean, it was cool! But I didn't even know general math. I immediately enrolled in night school where I was learning trigonometry and log rhythm scales. I had the books piled up and every time I needed to know something, I would hit the books. I was staying just an inch ahead of it all. Then they came to me one day and said, "You're one of the best draftsmen we've ever had here. Your drawings are so precise." What they didn't know was I'd already done that drawing twenty-two times while practicing at home, but I was determined to do it right.

If you're determined to back down the devil and put him where he's supposed to be, you can do it. You have the tools to do it. Just get determined and decide you're going to learn as you go. You can stay one step ahead of the devil. You've got the manual. That's what I did at this steel company. I had the manuals. When a job came up, everybody else may have been doing it without looking at the manuals, but I looked at the manuals. I had to spend extra time because I didn't know as much as they knew. But it was worth it because I wanted to keep my position.

The Devil is a Liar

When the devil comes against you and you don't know what to do, get out the manual and put in some overtime. Just determine you're going to do it. The devil may come at you with disappointment, depression, despair and discouragement. He likes to tell you all kinds of lies because he is a liar, but you don't have to listen to him.

> **You are of your father the devil; and it is your will to practice the lusts and gratify the desires [which are characteristic] of your father. He was a murderer from the beginning, and does not stand in the truth, because there is no truth in him. When he speaks a falsehood, he speaks what is natural to him; for he is a liar [himself] and the father of lies and of all that is false.**
>
> **John 8:44 (AMP)**

I've met people in my life who have lied to me. I choose not to listen to them anymore. Yet, I know people who will listen to someone who is a liar. You can't trust a liar. However, people still listen to them! I see people still listening to the lies of the devil and I think to myself, "Why in the world are they letting the devil convince them that they can be defeated?"

The Facts of Life

The scriptures give us the complete plan so we can access the provision God provides for us.

1. The blood represents life.

We know the blood represents life and is required for our atonement. Atonement is the foreshadow of redemption. In Leviticus 17:11 it says, *"For the life of the flesh is in the blood, and I have given it to you upon the altar to make atonement for your souls; for it is the blood that makes atonement for the soul."*

2. Christ redeemed us from the curse.

We know Ephesians 1:7 says that Christ redeemed us from the curse of the law by His blood because it says, *"In Him we have redemption through His blood, the forgiveness of sins..."*

3. We access the spirit realm through words of faith.

We access the spirit realm and apply the blood of Jesus through words of faith. Romans 10:8 says: *"But what does it say? 'The word is near you, in your mouth and in your heart' (that is, the word of faith which we preach)."* There is power in the Word, the name and the blood. The Word is near you. It is in your mouth!

Some people tell me, "When the devil is coming against me, I don't know what to say." Speaking the Word of God will set you free. The world has its own methods for freedom, but only God's method of putting His Word in your mouth and heart will defeat the devil. Psalm 91 is the kind of ammunition that will pick you up and set you on high places. It says:

> **He who dwells in the secret place of the Most High Shall abide under the shadow of the Almighty.**
>
> **I will say of the Lord, "He is my refuge and my fortress; My God, in Him I will trust."**
>
> **Psalm 91:1,2**

Did you notice that verse two says, *"I will say of the Lord"*? The scripture says you choose to claim what God says with your mouth.

> **Surely He shall deliver you from the snare of the fowler And from the perilous pestilence.**

He shall cover you with His feathers, And under His wings you shall take refuge; His truth shall be your shield and buckler.

You shall not be afraid of the terror by night, Nor of the arrow that flies by day,

Nor of the pestilence that walks in darkness, Nor of the destruction that lays waste at noonday.

A thousand may fall at your side, And ten thousand at your right hand; But it shall not come near you.

Only with your eyes shall you look, And see the reward of the wicked.

Because you have made the Lord, who is my refuge, Even the Most High, your dwelling place,

No evil shall befall you, Nor shall any plague come near your dwelling;

For He shall give His angels charge over you, To keep you in all your ways.

In their hands they shall bear you up, Lest you dash your foot against a stone.

You shall tread upon the lion and the cobra, The young lion and the serpent you shall trample underfoot.

"Because he has set his love upon Me, therefore I will deliver him; I will set him on high, because he has known My name.

"He shall call upon Me, and I will answer him; I will be with him in trouble; I will deliver him and honor him.

"With long life I will satisfy him, And show him My salvation."

Psalm 91:3-16

This is what God wants to do for you. Look carefully because this scripture tells you that God wants to protect you. It says God wants you to be set free. God wants to lift you up. This scripture promises that the angels will come and minister to you. It promises that God will be your shield and your buckler. It promises that when you're in trouble, God will be right there with you. He will take care of you. But verse two says, *"I will say."* You choose to claim and confess what God says is true with your mouth.

There is no distress with God because He's always here. He's our refuge. He promises to cover us with His wings. As long as we receive what He has for us by faith and acknowledge and stand upon it, there's nothing that can destroy us because the enemy would have to go through God to get to us and he can't.

Claiming the Blood Covenant

You access the protective power of Psalm 91 by speaking the blood covenant over your household. Some people may call this a "name it and claim it" or a "blab it and grab it" theology. They're right! We are responsible for what we claim and what we refuse to claim. We must know God's Word well enough to know what He wants us to have. Once we can "name" the promise, then we must "claim" the promise. To study the Word and know about the promises of God is not enough and will never set you free. Only when we acknowledge and act on His promise in faith will we bring it into reality for us.

Psalm 91 is the same kind of protection that the Hebrews had when they put the blood on the doorpost. But we have a better covenant. We don't have to kill a lamb or go through a ritual. We have only to believe in and speak the blood of Jesus and the blood of Jesus goes onto the door of our house to protect us. Don't you think that sounds like a better covenant? Here are six steps that cover all we need to do as Christians to access the power.

First, you become righteous. You do that by getting saved.

Second, once you're saved, you abide in His Word.

Third, you speak your heart. If you're abiding in His Word, what you speak from your heart will be His Word.

Fourth, you develop a lifestyle of faith. This is an important step. I call it "walking in holiness".

Fifth, you access the spirit realm in the name and by the blood of Jesus through the words of your mouth.

Sixth, you get ready to receive because miracles are about to happen.

Controlling the Tongue

James 1:26 says, *"If anyone among you thinks he is religious, and does not bridle his tongue but deceives his own heart, this one's religion is useless."* Your mouth can cause you to make your religion useless. You can go to church every week and be a Bible scholar, but if your mouth is speaking envy, strife and hatred, your mouth will cause your religion to be worthless. You do not access the spirit realm and the throne of God with your religion. You access the spirit realm and the throne of God with your words of faith.

Second Corinthians 4:13 says, *"And since we have the same spirit of faith, according to what is written, 'I believed and therefore I spoke,' we also believe and therefore speak."* The spirit of faith operates this way. You believe it, and you speak it. You are going to speak what you really believe. That is why it is so important to watch the words of your mouth and the meditations of your heart (Psalm 19:14).

Let me tell you about an incident I saw. A Christian lady approached another Christian lady for prayer. She prayed what appeared to be a prayer of faith. A few moments later I heard the lady who prayed tell another person that the lady she had just prayed for was in great pain and needed to be healed. She also told that person to continue praying so that the lady would be healed.

This is a great example of how a prayer can appear to be in faith, but not be. Faith is in the heart and the mouth. A confession or prayer without belief in the heart is not a faith confession or a prayer of faith. A positive confession is good, but a confession of faith is where the power is.

Did you follow what happened here? A few minutes ago, this sister had prayed for this lady to be healed in the name of Jesus. The Word says, if we pray in faith, we are to believe we have received what we prayed for. But within moments, her confession was that the lady she prayed for was in a lot of pain and still needed healing. Without saying it directly, she confessed that healing had not taken place.

What does this mean? It means when it came down to it, the person who was praying didn't really believe in her heart that God had done what she prayed for Him to do. Out of the abundance of her heart, her mouth eventually spoke.

If we aren't careful, we could find ourselves doing the same thing. What we say we are believing for, we could unconsciously deny with our own words. What we're doing may not be clear to other Christians, but God sees the whole situation. When we are believing for something, we may be affirming and confirming our faith one moment and later denying it without really saying we're denying it by the way we use our words.

The devil very subtly tempts us to use our words to nullify our faith. God wants you to agree with the Word, but the devil wants you to agree with his lies.

Believing What We Speak

Apply the blood of Jesus over your own household. Don't expect your pastor or an elder in your church to come over and apply the blood of Jesus for you. You believe in the power of the blood, so...speak it!

The scripture doesn't say Moses went and applied the blood to every household during the Passover. Moses didn't run around to every Hebrew house, knock on the door and say, "Have you applied the blood yet? You haven't? Well, would you feel better if I did it?" No! Each household was responsible for applying the blood to their own household.

It's one thing to sit here and read about the power of the blood, but it's something else to actually apply it. Knowing about the blood, thinking about the blood, knowing people who apply the blood and even extensive study about the blood will profit you nothing until you stand up in faith and actually apply the blood.

When I get up in the morning, the first thing I do is apply the blood over everyone and everything in my household. I put Jesus' blood over my wife, my household, my children and their possessions, the church membership and our church building. Do you see what I mean? Words — that's how we apply the blood under the new covenant.

When we apply the blood, no evil spirit being has access. The devil is a spirit being. He is defeated in the spirit realm because that's where he lives. If we could see into the spirit realm, I believe we would see the blood of Jesus is a real substance of protection and it causes the destroyer to pass by.

What We Say Affects What We Get

Now faith is the substance of things hoped for, the evidence of things not seen.

Hebrews 11:1

We don't naturally see faith, but in the spirit realm faith can be seen. I believe when we pass over into the spirit realm, we will be shocked at the things we have moved around over there by the words of our mouth.

Over the years I've heard many people make the comment, "It doesn't matter what you say. It only matters what you do." What we do is extremely important. We know that faith without works is dead. However, we cannot ignore the value and power of our words. Our words are our commitment to our decision that we make in our soul. Yes, actions are important, but if our words don't line up with our actions and our words don't change, our actions will.

Again, if a man is a good husband who treats his wife well, but he constantly speaks to everyone else that she is lazy, ugly, worthless and stupid, and if he refuses to change his confession and continues to speak these bad words about his wife, he will eventually start to believe his own words. As this happens, his outward actions will start lining up with what he speaks and believes. His words will change his actions.

Everybody has 20/20 hindsight. If you would have known 20 years ago what you know now, I'm sure many disasters would have been avoided. However, don't get caught in the trap of looking backward. Look forward in faith. Change your words starting today.

God Listens to Your Words

God listens to your words. In Deuteronomy chapter 1 it says,

The Lord your God, who goes before you, He will fight for you, according to all He did for you in Egypt before your eyes.

And in the wilderness where you saw how the Lord your God carried you, as a man carries his son, in all the way that you went until you came to this place.

Yet for all that, you did not believe the Lord your God,

who went in the way before you to search out a place for you to pitch your tents, to show you the way you should go, in the fire by night and in the cloud by day.

Deuteronomy 1:30-33

God did miraculous things for His people! However, I want you to particularly note what is said in verse 34.

And the Lord heard the sound of your words, and was angry...

Deuteronomy 1:34

God hears our words. Our words can please Him or they can make Him angry. Do you think it's better to please God or make Him angry?

Read the story about Sodom and Gomorrah. They made God angry. Read about the Hebrews who grumbled in their tents. The scripture said that God heard their words and got angry. It resulted in them wandering around in the wilderness for forty years. Not a single person who grumbled entered the Promised Land. They all died in the wilderness because of the words of their mouths.

If you want to please God, you must take heed of Hebrews 11:6: *"Without faith it's impossible to please God."* We please God by believing what He says and speaking it. He has given us everything we need to defeat the power of sin in our lives with the words of our mouths and actions following.

Chapter 8
The Power to Defeat Sin

Most people live their lives trying to defeat sin. This may come as a shock to some people, but born-again believers are without sin. The Word of God says in 1 John 3:9, *"Whoever has been born of God does not sin, for His seed remains in him; and he cannot sin, because he has been born of God."*

When people read the scripture in Romans 3:23 that says, *"for all have sinned and fall short of the glory of God,"* they wonder how these two scriptures fit together.

Here's how it works. Yes, you were born into sin. That means you were born with a sin nature. The spirit within you desired to sin because you were without God.

When you accepted Jesus Christ as your Lord and Savior, 2 Corinthians 5:17 tells us that old things passed away and all things became new in Christ. Your spirit was born of God's Spirit. That is when 1 John 3:9 began to apply to you: *"Whoever is born of God does not sin...he cannot sin because he has been born of God."*

If that's the case, most people want to know why there is such a battle with sin? If our spirit now desires to do right, why is there still an urge to sin? Here's the answer. We are three-part beings. We are body, soul and spirit. The real you is spirit. That is the part that was born again. But your mind is something you must renew on a daily basis.

> **Do not be conformed to this world — this age, fashioned after and adapted to its external, superficial customs. But be transformed (changed) by the [entire] renewal of your mind — by its new ideals and its new attitude — so that you may prove [for yourselves] what is the good and acceptable and perfect will of God, even the thing which is good and acceptable and perfect [in His sight for you].**
>
> **Romans 12:2 (AMP)**

Renewing your mind is a continual process. It will never end as long as you live on this earth.

The good fight of faith talked about in 1 Timothy 6:12 is fought in the battlefield of the mind. The Word of God says you have only one fight to fight and that's the good fight of faith. The mind is the place where the words of God do battle with the words of the devil. You must decide which words to accept and which words to reject. A Christian should reject words which represent vain imaginations and evil thoughts. Second Corinthians 10:4,5 says you must cast them down.

> **For the weapons of our warfare *are* not carnal but mighty in God for pulling down strongholds,**
>
> **casting down arguments and every high thing that exalts itself against the knowledge of God, bringing every thought into captivity to the obedience of Christ.**
>
> **2 Corinthians 10:4,5**

The words you keep are the words you're going to meditate on. They will get into your heart. And out of the abundance of your heart, your mouth speaks (Matthew 12:34). As the Word of God gets into your mind, it becomes easier to know which words to accept and which to reject. Then when the Word of God comes out of your mouth, you will be speaking faith.

Knowing How Sin Works

If defeating sin is a problem for you, it is important to understand what sin is and how it works against you. Then, you can apply the blood of Jesus and defeat this problem.

First of all, let's define sin. Sin is anything that is opposed to the will or the Word of God. So, anything that is not of faith is sin.

> **But he who doubts is condemned if he eats, because *he does* not *eat* from faith; for whatever is not from faith is sin.**
>
> **Romans 14:23**

The Word of God says it is sin any time we doubt God, worry or fret because we don't think He can handle our problems.

> **For in it the righteousness of God is revealed from faith to faith; as it is written, "The just shall live by faith."**
>
> **Romans 1:17**

Next, let's define faith. If the just shall live by faith, then we need to know what faith is. Faith is the simple belief that God has done what He said He would do, and everything you say and do is based on that belief. That's faith. So any time we don't believe God has done what He said He would do, it's sin.

Jesus says in John 10:10, *"The thief does not come except to steal, and to kill, and to destroy. I have come that they may have life, and that they may have it more abundantly."*

The thief wants to steal, kill, and destroy. The way he does that is by getting you to sin. When you sin, you're turning your back on God and His protective power. Sin opens the door for the devil to come in and wreak havoc upon you and your family.

How to Stop the Attack of Sin

So, how do we stop this attack of sin? You choose to believe the Word of God. If God's Word says He will heal you, but you don't believe it, that's sin. If God's Word says He will deliver you but you don't believe it, that's sin. If God's Word says He will prosper you, but you don't believe it, that's sin. In fact, when you don't believe what God says, you are calling Him a liar. That is never faith. That is always sin.

Coming Out of Darkness

You are the light of the world. A city that is set on a hill cannot be hidden.

Matthew 5:14

We are called to be the light of the world. Light always overpowers darkness. God is light. The devil represents the darkness of this world.

This is the message which we have heard from Him and declare to you, that God is light and in Him is no darkness at all.

1 John 1:5

To open their eyes, *in order* to turn *them* from darkness to light, and *from* the power of Satan to God, that they may receive forgiveness of sins and an inheritance among those who are sanctified by faith in Me.

Acts 26:18

Look at Matthew 27:45. *"Now from the sixth hour until the ninth hour there was darkness over all the land."*

For three hours there was darkness everywhere while Jesus was hanging on the cross. Matthew 27:46

says, *"About the ninth hour Jesus cried out with a loud voice, saying,...'My God, my God, why have You forsaken Me?'"*

When Jesus took our sin upon Himself, God turned His back on Him. Why? Because God cannot look upon sin. That is why we must be light. We must be forgiven. If we walk in darkness, God cannot look upon us.

Darkness represents sin. Satan is the prince of darkness, but God is the light that overpowers darkness. If it's pitch dark outside and the lights are turned on inside, the light illuminates the room and even goes through the windows to expose darkness outside. Why? Because wherever there's light, the darkness has to flee. It doesn't work the other way around. You can never overpower light with darkness.

Think about it. Everyone knows what a flashlight is. But have you ever heard of a "flashdark?" Have you ever seen a device you could carry around during the day and when you would turn it on and point it into a room, it would make the room dark? Of course not! There is no such thing as a "flashdark." That's because light always overpowers darkness and where there is light, darkness cannot dispel it. The only way to have darkness is through the absence of light.

Jesus took our sin because we could not come into the presence of God with sin. Light and darkness do not mix. 1 John 1 says:

> **If we say we have fellowship with Him, and walk in darkness, we lie and do not practice the truth.**
>
> **But if we walk in the light as He is in the light, we have fellowship with one another, and the blood of Jesus Christ His Son cleanses us from all sin."**
>
> **If we say that we have no sin, we deceive ourselves, and the truth is not in us.**

If we confess our sins, He is faithful and just to forgive us our sins and to cleanse us from all righteousness.

If we say that we have not sinned, we make Him a liar, and His word is not in us.

1 John 1:6-8

Notice in verse 7 the scripture doesn't say "some of the sin." It says the blood of Jesus Christ cleanses us from *all* sin. Without the blood we cannot stand before God and say we're not sinners. We were born into this world as sinners. But, when we accept Jesus, we become a new creature in Christ. Then, 1 John 3:9 applies to us, *"Whoever has been born of God does not sin...because He has been born of God."*

If life is in the blood, you will not have spiritual life until the blood of Jesus cleanses you from all sin. Then you can stand before the Father and talk to Him because you are without sin.

In the Old Testament, the people had to have an earthly priest in order to talk to God. But in the New Testament, the Word of God says that once we've accepted Jesus as our Lord and Savior, we can go directly to the Father using the name of Jesus.

If the blood of Jesus hasn't cleansed us, we cannot approach God and expect to be heard because God cannot look upon sinful man. We must be washed in the blood. If we ignore the blood, we cannot approach God.

God doesn't change. So, when He sets a pattern, we're to imitate Him as it says in Ephesians 5:1: *"Therefore be imitators of God as dear children."*

God set up a pattern which later became a law for the Hebrews and the basis of the blood covenant for us. The foundation of this principle begins in Genesis chapter 3:

So when the woman saw that the tree was good for food, that it was pleasant to the eyes, and a tree desirable to make one wise, she took of its fruit and ate. She also gave to her husband with her, and he ate.

Then the eyes of both of them were opened, and they knew that they were naked; and they sewed fig leaves together and made themselves coverings.

And they heard the sound of the Lord God walking in the garden in the cool of the day, and Adam and his wife hid themselves from the presence of the Lord God among the trees of the garden.

Then the Lord God called to Adam and said to him, "Where are you?"

So he said, "I heard Your voice in the garden, and I was afraid because I was naked; and I hid myself."

Genesis 3:6-10

Notice in verse 7 that Adam and Eve made their own coverings to hide their nakedness. When God came, He called to them even though He knew where they were. When Adam answered and told God he was hiding because he was naked, he was actually lying. He had just made a covering for himself so he would not be naked. Yet, Adam knew in his heart that he was still naked in God's eyes because the covering of the glory was gone.

And He said, "Who told you that you were naked? Have you eaten from the tree of which I commanded you that you should not eat?"

Then the man said, "The woman whom You gave to be with me, she gave me of the tree, and I ate."

Genesis 3:11,12

That's right, blame the woman!

And the Lord God said to the woman, "What is this you have done?" The woman said, "The serpent deceived me, and I ate."

Genesis 3:13

That's right, blame the devil!

So the Lord God said to the serpent: "Because you have done this, You are cursed more than all cattle, And more than every beast of the field; On your belly you shall go, And you shall eat dust All the days of your life.

"And I will put enmity between you and the woman, And between your seed and her Seed; He shall bruise your head, And you shall bruise His heel."

To the woman He said: "I will greatly multiply your sorrow and your conception; In pain you shall bring forth children. Your desire shall be for your husband, And he shall rule over you."

Genesis 3:14-16

God didn't say He would create sorrow and conception. He said He would multiply them. He also didn't say the woman was going to start bringing forth children. He said Eve would have pain in bringing forth children.

Then to Adam He said, "Because you have heeded the voice of your wife, and have eaten of which I commanded you, saying, 'You shall not eat of it': Cursed is the ground for your sake; In toil you shall eat of it all the days of your life.

"Both thorns and thistles it shall bring forth for you, and you shall eat the herb of the field."

Genesis 3:17,18

Here is the place where man's prosperity became cursed, but Jesus broke that curse when the thorns were put on His brow.

"In the sweat of your face you shall eat bread till you return to the ground, for out of it you were taken; for dust you are, and to dust you shall return."

And Adam called his wife's name Eve, because she was the mother of all living.

Also for Adam and his wife the Lord made tunics of skin, and clothed them.

Genesis 3:19-21

This is what I want you to understand. Adam made clothing out of what was grown from the earth. But this wasn't an acceptable covering to God or He wouldn't have turned right around and killed an animal to make clothing out of the skin. In order to have the correct covering, an animal had to shed its blood.

Remember, God requires blood for atonement. Again, in Leviticus 17:11 it says, *"For the life of the flesh is in the blood, and I have given it to you upon the altar to make atonement for your souls; for it is the blood that makes atonement for the soul."* God's laws are God's laws regardless of whether or not people understand them or receive them.

God sets up a pattern in Genesis that we can follow throughout the scriptures. Some day we will totally understand why we have all the spiritual idiosyncrasies of these rules, but until then, the bottom line is we either choose to obey them or we don't.

Choosing Life

In Deuteronomy 30:19, the Word says, *"...I have set before you life and death...therefore choose life."*

Let's look at Genesis 4 to see the importance of choosing to obey God and correctly applying the blood.

Now Adam knew Eve his wife, and she conceived and bore Cain, and said, "I have acquired a man from the Lord."

Then she bore again, this time his brother Abel. Now Abel was a keeper of sheep, but Cain was a tiller of the ground.

And in the process of time it came to pass that Cain brought an offering of the fruit of the ground.

Genesis 4:1-3

Look at what God is showing us here. Abel was a keeper of something that contained blood. Cain was a tiller and a keeper of something that was cursed. Remember, the ground had been cursed. We could paraphrase verse 3 to read "And in the process of time it came to pass that Cain brought an offering from the ground that God had cursed." Notice what Abel brought.

Abel also brought of the firstborn of his flock and of their fat. And the Lord respected Abel and his offering.

But He did not respect Cain and his offering. And Cain was very angry, and his countenance fell.

So the Lord said to Cain, "Why are you angry? And why has your countenance fallen?

"If you do well, will you not be accepted? And if you do not do well, sin lies at the door. And its desire is for you, but you should rule over it."

Genesis 4:4-7

Cain brought an offering that was cursed and God did not accept it. If we were to paraphrase verse 7, we could say, "If you give the right offering and apply the blood, will you not be accepted? But if you don't give the right offering and don't apply the blood, sin lies at the door."

We are told here that we should rule over sin. It waits at the door for us. We **can** rule over the sin that is waiting at the door if we follow the type and shadow of Abel. But, if we offer an offering after the type and shadow of Cain, we can expect sin to overtake us. Cain and Abel both knew what was required to please God. Cain simply chose not to do it. God had already substituted the clothing of Adam and Eve with a covering that required the shedding of blood for their sin. The Word shows us that it is God's plan that blood makes atonement for the soul.

God's Method for Defeating Sin

Now Cain talked with Abel his brother; and it came to pass, when they were in the field, that Cain rose up against Abel his brother and killed him.

Genesis 4:8

Any time sin is committed, it takes the applying of blood for the atonement or remission of sin, according to the Word of God. It started in the Garden of Eden. When Adam and Eve sinned, God provided a covering by shedding the blood of an animal. The word atonement actually means "to cover." Cain knew his brother's sacrifice was accepted. Cain simply rejected what God said. He decided the ground was good enough. But God's way says it takes blood to make atonement for sin.

God had warned Cain that if he did not do well, sin was ready to overtake him. In verse 9, God approached Cain after Cain had killed his brother.

Then the Lord said to Cain, "Where is Abel your brother?" He said, "I do not know. Am I my brother's keeper?"

And He said, "What have you done? The voice of your brother's blood cries out to Me from the ground."

Genesis 4:9,10

Life is in the blood. Look at what Jesus said about Abel in Matthew chapter 23.

> **Therefore, indeed, I send you prophets, wise men, and scribes: some of them you will kill and crucify, and some of them you will scourge in your synagogues and persecute from city to city,**
>
> **that on you may come all the righteous blood shed on the earth, from the blood of righteous Abel to the blood of Zechariah....**
>
> **Matthew 23:34,35**

Jesus called Abel righteous. He was made righteous because God recognized the blood as a righteous sacrifice.

This is the same law God gave to the Hebrews through Moses. The way they applied the blood under the old covenant was to physically kill an animal. The way we apply the blood of Jesus under the new covenant is by the words we speak. Our faith in the shed blood of Jesus and the Word of God is what's required under the new covenant.

The sacrifice of Abel was better than Cain's. Hebrews 11:4 says, *"By faith Abel offered to God a more excellent sacrifice than Cain, through which he obtained witness that he was righteous, God testifying of his gifts; and through it he being dead still speaks."* Abel was alive and remained alive through his blood. Under the new covenant we receive everlasting life and remain alive for all eternity through the blood of Jesus.

In Hebrews 12:24 it says, *"To Jesus the Mediator of the new covenant, and to the blood of sprinkling that speaks better things than that of Abel."* The blood of Jesus is much more powerful than the blood of Abel or that of bulls and goats. Under the new covenant, the blood of Jesus is the only thing that remits sin. Matthew 26:28 says, *"For this is My blood of the new covenant which is shed for many for the remission of sins."*

Now remission is different than covering. Under the old covenant, the shedding of the blood of bulls and goats atoned or covered the sin. The sin wasn't gone, it was just covered.

A good illustration is when somebody unexpectedly shows up at your house. You take all the mess and clutter and you throw it in the closet. The house isn't really cleaned, the junk is just hidden. But the blood of Jesus cleans us. Sin is gone. When the blood of Jesus cleanses your house (your heart), you can open up every drawer and every closet because the hidden places have no junk (sin) and they are clean. When you clean your house, you do the best you can and try to make it look clean. When Jesus cleans your house, everything is 100% spotless. A speck of dust does not exist.

Defeating Sin — Once and for All

Without the shedding of blood there is no remission of sin. Hebrews 9:22 says, *"And according to the law almost all things are purified with blood, and without the shedding of blood there is no remission."* 1 John 1:6,7 says, *"If we say we have fellowship with Him, and walk in darkness, we lie and do not practice the truth. But if we walk in the light as He is in the light, we have fellowship with one another, and the blood of Jesus Christ His Son cleanses us from all sin."*

You do not have any rooms hidden away in your heart with the door locked anymore. Every room is clean. You don't have hidden sin anymore. It's gone by the applying of the blood. Hebrews 9:26 says, *"He then would have had to suffer often since the foundation of the world; but now, once at the end of the ages, He has appeared to put away sin by the sacrifice of Himself."* Jesus came to earth so that by the sacrifice of Himself, He put away sin once and for all. It's gone forever.

There is no reason why we should have to spend our lives trying to defeat sin. Just apply the blood of Jesus and the sin is gone. You do it all by the words of your mouth. That's the way we apply the blood now. So, if you have a problem with pornography, you say, "Father, in the name of Jesus, I apply the blood of Jesus to my mind. I will not think those thoughts anymore. I hold up Jesus' blood as a barrier between pornography and me. I am protected by the blood of Jesus." Speak the word of faith and act on it and you will stop the sin in your life.

The blood of Jesus is a barrier to the destroyer in the same way today as it was when the blood of the lambs was applied to the doorpost under the old covenant. The destroyer may come, but when he gets to your house, he must pass over. That's why God had the Hebrew children call it the "Passover."

You can be experiencing the joy of the Passover every day. When you get up in the morning, apply the blood of Jesus to yourself, to your spouse, over your house, over your children and over your possessions and everything that is important to you.

It works the same way today as it worked then, only better. The blood of bulls and goats covered sin, but the blood of Jesus remits it. Speaking the blood of Jesus is God's way of doing things under the new covenant. *"And since we have the same spirit of faith, according to what is written, 'I believed and therefore I spoke,' we also believe and therefore speak"* (2 Corinthians 4:13). When you believe it, speak it and act on it — it happens.

Chapter 9
Jesus is the Door

Let's examine how Jesus is the Passover Lamb. In Leviticus 23:4 it says,

> **These *are* the feasts of the LORD, holy convocations which you shall proclaim at their appointed times.**
>
> **On the fourteenth *day* of the first month at twilight *is* the Lord's Passover.**
>
> **Leviticus 23:4,5**

The Passover represents and memorializes the deliverance of the Hebrews out of slavery in Egypt. For approximately 430 years, the Hebrews had been in Egypt in slavery and in bondage. God called Moses to deliver His people out of slavery and out of bondage and into the promised land or the land of promise. That's what God has done today for you. God has called you out of the land of bondage, out of the land of slavery and into the land of promise. God has a covenant that He has made with you and He has signed that covenant in the blood of His Son, Jesus.

In Old Testament times, God also had a covenant with man. The word *testament* means covenant, agreement or contract. This was called the old covenant, or the old agreement. When Jesus showed up on the scene, He did not come to destroy the old covenant. However,

He came to give us better promises based on a better covenant.

> **Do not think that I came to destroy the Law or the Prophets. I did not come to destroy but to fulfill.**
>
> **Matthew 5:17**

The Promises are Not the Covenant

The promises of God are not the covenant of God. Sometimes people get that confused. We have an agreement, a covenant, and on the foundation of that covenant there are promises. In the old covenant, there were promises and under the new covenant, there are promises. But we have, according to the Word of God, a better set of promises based on a better covenant because of the blood of Jesus.

During the time when the Hebrews were delivered out of Egypt, they were delivered out of Egypt as a result of the power of the blood of the physical lambs that were slain. They had a problem when they were in Egypt. The problem was this: Pharaoh would not let them leave.

Remember the movie, "The Ten Commandments?" Well, that movie is loosely based on the Word of God, but there are some truths in it. The bottom line is this: God told Moses, "Take My people out of Egypt and into the land of promise." Moses went to Pharaoh and said, "Let my people go." Pharaoh said, "No, I will not let your people go." Moses then proclaimed that God would put a plague on the land unless the people were released. Pharaoh would not agree. So, the plague hit the land of Egypt. Everybody was distraught. However, Pharaoh hardened his heart all the more and refused to let God's people go. Over and over through these plagues the people were not allowed to leave Egypt until the tenth plague.

In Exodus 8:15 it says,

But when Pharaoh saw that there was relief, he hardened his heart and did not heed them, as the LORD had said.

Exodus 8:15

So Pharaoh's heart was hardened and the plagues just kept on coming.

Here is a listing of the ten plagues:

1. The water of the Nile River turned into blood. (Exodus 7:19-21)

2. Frogs overran the countryside. (Exodus 8:5,6)

3. Lice infested man and animals. (Exodus 8:16,17)

4. Swarms of flies covered the land. (Exodus 8:24)

5. Disease killed the livestock of Egypt. (Exodus 9:6)

6. Boils and sores infected the Egyptians and their animals. (Exodus 9:8-10)

7. Hail destroyed crops and vegetation. (Exodus 9:22-26)

8. Swarms of locusts covered the land. (Exodus 10:12-15)

9. Darkness covered Egypt for three days. (Exodus 10:21-23)

10. The Egyptian firstborn and the firstborn of all those in Egypt, both people and their animals, were destroyed by God's death angel. (Exodus 12:29,30)

The tenth plague is the one that knocked Egypt and Pharaoh to their knees. The tenth plague caused great mourning in all of Egypt. Pharaoh finally said, "You've been wanting to go? Go!"

Character Creates Favor

And the LORD said to Moses, "I will bring yet one *more* plague on Pharaoh and on Egypt. Afterward

he will let you go from here. When he lets *you* go, he will surely drive you out of here altogether.

"Speak now in the hearing of the people, and let every man ask from his neighbor and every woman from her neighbor, articles of silver and articles of gold."

And the LORD gave the people favor in the sight of the Egyptians. Moreover the man Moses *was* very great in the land of Egypt, in the sight of Pharaoh's servants and in the sight of the people.

Then Moses said, "Thus says the LORD: 'About midnight I will go out into the midst of Egypt;

'and all the firstborn in the land of Egypt shall die, from the firstborn of Pharaoh who sits on his throne, even to the firstborn of the female servant who is behind the handmill, and all the firstborn of the animals.'"

Exodus 11:1-5

Basically, here's what happened. God said to Moses, "I want you to have all the men and all the women go to their neighbors and borrow all the articles of silver and of gold that they have." Because Moses had favor with the people who worked for Pharaoh and the people of Egypt, the people of Israel could go out and get whatever they wanted.

Favor in your life is an important thing. Too many Christians have the idea of "in your face, buddy" and push their Christianity in such a way that they become obnoxious and appear arrogant. Because of this, they shut themselves off from having any influence on the world whatsoever.

Moses had character. Because of his character, his reliability and the honesty of his word, he had favor with the servants of Pharaoh and the people of Egypt. When it came time to tap into that favor to get what God told him to get, they didn't write him off as a looney. So, don't be deceived. The devil would like nothing more than for you to be considered a lunatic.

Yes, we are peculiar. The people of Egypt probably thought Moses was peculiar because of some of the things he did. You may seem peculiar in the eyes of the world, but still have character and favor. Never, never throw away your character. It is one of your best witnessing tools.

Silver and Gold

God told the Hebrews to get all the silver and gold. They took it to their houses. God also said He was sending a plague and this plague would kill the first-born of every household. But, God is a God of mercy and a God of grace. He always makes a way of escape for His people.

Look at Noah and the ark. Because of the vileness of the people of that day, God decided He was going to destroy the earth with water. However, for those eight people who believed in God and were obedient to God and did what God said to do, they were not destroyed. They were delivered out of the flood waters. God has always made a way of escape for His people.

> **And did not spare the ancient world, but saved Noah, one of eight people, a preacher of righteousness, bringing in the flood on the world of the ungodly.**
>
> **2 Peter 2:5**

The Word tells us in the New Testament that God is never going to allow you to be tempted with something beyond your ability to stand. In the temptation He will always make a way of escape.

> **No temptation has overtaken you except such as is common to man; but God is faithful, who will not allow you to be tempted beyond what you are able,**

but with the temptation will also make the way of escape, that you may be able to bear it.

1 Corinthians 10:13

That way of escape has to do with obedience. Obedience is a word that makes some people cringe. Many people want to do whatever it is they want to do, whenever they want to do it.

Once a man told me, "I live in the land of the free and the home of the brave. I am an American. Nobody is going to tell me what to do. I'm going to do what I want to do, when I want to do it and don't you tell me otherwise." There are a lot of attitudes like that. Part of the reason is because of the massive amount of freedom that we have. We must remember, as Christians, we live in a kingdom. In a kingdom, you do what the king says to do and you do it when He says to do it. In a kingdom the king rules. As Christians we do not live in a democracy, but in a kingdom.

The Tenth Plague

God gave specific instructions on what to do to be set free from the tenth plague. God proclaimed there would be judgment because of disobedience and God said that the firstborn of every household would die. He then detailed a procedure that would stop the death angel from coming into their homes and wreaking havoc in their lives.

Let's look at these instructions in Exodus chapter 12.

Now the LORD spoke to Moses and Aaron in the land of Egypt, saying,

"This month *shall be* your beginning of months; it *shall be* the first month of the year to you.

"Speak to all the congregation of Israel, saying: 'On the tenth *day* of this month every man shall take

for himself a lamb, according to the house of *his* father, a lamb for a household.

'And if the household is too small for the lamb, let him and his neighbor next to his house take *it* according to the number of the persons; according to each man's need you shall make your count for the lamb.

'Your lamb shall be without blemish, a male of the first year. You may take *it* from the sheep or from the goats.

'Now you shall keep it until the fourteenth day of the same month. Then the whole assembly of the congregation of Israel shall kill it at twilight.

'And they shall take *some* of the blood and put *it* on the two doorposts and on the lintel of the houses where they eat it.

'Then they shall eat the flesh on that night; roasted in fire, with unleavened bread *and* with bitter *herbs* they shall eat it.

'Do not eat it raw, nor boiled at all with water, but roasted in fire; its head with its legs and its entrails.

'You shall let none of it remain until morning, and what remains of it until morning you shall burn with fire.

'And thus you shall eat it: *with* a belt on your waist, your sandals on your feet, and your staff in your hand. So you shall eat it in haste. It *is* the Lord's Passover.

'For I will pass through the land of Egypt on that night, and will strike all the firstborn in the land of Egypt, both man and beast; and against all the gods of Egypt I will execute judgment: I *am* the LORD.

'Now the blood shall be a sign for you on the houses where you *are*. And when I see the blood, I

will pass over you; and the plague shall not be on you to destroy *you* when I strike the land of Egypt.

'So this day shall be to you a memorial; and you shall keep it as a feast to the LORD throughout your generations. You shall keep it as a feast by an everlasting ordinance.'"

Exodus 12:1-14

The Hebrews followed these directions to the letter. Because they followed the directions and put the blood of the lamb on the doorposts and the lintel, when the death angel came to their house, the death angel did not enter. The death angel passed over and went on to the next house. If there was blood on the doorposts of that house, it passed over that house also. When the death angel would get to a house where there was no blood on the doorpost, then he entered in and took the firstborn of the household and the firstborn of the animals. The next morning, according to the Word of God and according to history, there was a great cry throughout the land of Egypt. There was great mourning. It was horrible. From the house of Pharaoh on down to the house of the servants, God's judgment struck the land of Egypt.

And so, the Hebrews were released. Exodus 12:14 says, *"So this day shall be to you a memorial..."* It was set aside as a day to remember the deliverance of the Hebrews out of Egypt. It was called the Passover.

For one thousand five hundred years, the Hebrews celebrated the Passover on the fourteenth day of the month. During that time there were prophets of God that were raised up. The prophets of God would speak and say, "There is a Lamb coming and He will be the Messiah. He will be the Deliverer of Israel." These prophecies were plain for everyone to see. The Jews knew what was going to happen. They started looking for a Messiah that would fit the qualifications. But just like people today, sometimes things become so traditional that we overlook the obvious. They began to do things by rote instead of by heart.

Exodus 12:47 is a command that God told Moses and Aaron. He said all the congregation shall keep it. It was a command that they keep the Passover. There are some things that happened when they sacrificed the lamb before they went out of Egypt at that first Passover. Here is a brief overview of what happened.

1. Each man was to select a lamb without spot or blemish and he was to select it on the 10th day of the month.

2. He was to observe this lamb for five days to make sure that this lamb was without spot or blemish and that it had no fault in it.

3. On the fifth day he was to take the lamb to the doorpost and he was to kill it.

4. He was to catch the blood in a basin.

5. He was supposed to sprinkle the blood on the doorpost and above the doorpost, completely covering the entrance to his home with the blood of the sacrificed lamb.

6. This was to be done on the evening of the 14th day at twilight.

God's Timing

Let me say this. God gives us specific instructions on when to do things in our lives. I've had people tell me, "God called me to be a missionary." "God called me to be a pastor." "God called me to be an evangelist." "God called me to go witness to my neighbor and I am going to, just as soon as I get my life in order." Wait a minute. If God has told you to wait until you get your life in order, that's fine. However, postponed obedience is disobedience.

We have so many excuses. When God tells you to do something at a certain time, you don't do it beforehand and you don't do it afterward. You do it when God says to do it. The only way you are going to be obedient is to do what God says to do, when He says to do it. Some people are doing what God said, but they are doing it in the wrong time. When you have one Christian in the body of believers who is out of step time-wise, it can create confusion.

I know God told me to start a church in Osage Beach. But the key was, I had to do it when He wanted it done. Had I tried to do it fifteen years earlier, it would have been a flop. Why? It wasn't God's timing fifteen years earlier. But, in my natural mind I can think things like, "Well, I sure would have been a lot younger." That's a brilliant deduction. I wonder what kind of lightning fast brain had to figure that out? Would you have been younger fifteen years ago? Possibly so.

We have excuses and reasons for everything. We need to understand Jesus was very patient. For thirty years of His life here on the earth, He was the Son of Man and the Son of God. He was God. He said, "If you've seen Me, you've seen the Father." For thirty years He patiently waited for that moment when the Holy Spirit would descend upon Him and the voice from heaven would say, "This is My Son in Whom I am well pleased." At the point that He was empowered with the Holy Spirit, His ministry started and for three years He and a band of unique followers turned this world upside down. Jesus said He didn't say or do anything unless the Father told Him to. Not only did He say and do what the Father said to say and do, He did it in the Father's timing according to the Father's plan. What if Jesus had decided at the age of 27 to get a three year jump start on His ministry. He would have been in disobedience and He wouldn't have been the perfect Lamb.

Jesus in Prophecy

For fifteen hundred years the Jews celebrated the Passover and they understood what the Passover meant. Then Jesus was sent here to earth as the sacrificial Lamb. Let's look at what the prophet Isaiah said in Isaiah 53.

> **Surely He has borne our griefs And carried our sorrows; Yet we esteemed Him stricken, Smitten by God, and afflicted.**
>
> **But He *was* wounded for our transgressions, *He was* bruised for our iniquities; The chastisement for our peace *was* upon Him, And by His stripes we are healed.**
>
> **All we like sheep have gone astray; We have turned, every one, to his own way; And the LORD has laid on Him the iniquity of us all.**
>
> **He was oppressed and He was afflicted, Yet He opened not His mouth; He was led as a lamb to the slaughter, And as a sheep before its shearers is silent, So He opened not His mouth.**
>
> **He was taken from prison and from judgment, And who will declare His generation? For He was cut off from the land of the living; For the transgressions of My people He was stricken.**
>
> **And they made His grave with the wicked; But with the rich at His death, Because He had done no violence, Nor *was any* deceit in His mouth.**
>
> **Isaiah 53:4-9**

When we are talking about the purity of Jesus in prophecy and the purity of the Lamb, I think it is key to understand that it was prophesied there was no deceit in His mouth. The Word tells us that death and life are in the power of the tongue. Jesus said we will be judged by our words. So, the words of the Messiah were very important to the prophet Isaiah and of course very important to God.

As the fifteen hundred years came to a close and Jesus was born here on this earth, another prophet, John the Baptist, prophesied that the Lamb of God was coming. In John 1:29 he said, *"Behold the Lamb of God Who takes away the sin of the world."* In John 1:35,36 it says, *"Again, the next day, John stood with two of his disciples. And looking at Jesus as He walked, he said, 'Behold the Lamb of God!'"*

The Passover Lamb

Jesus was set aside to be sacrificed, examined, tested and crucified on the exact month, day and hour that the Jews had been handling and slaughtering the lambs for over fifteen hundred years in the keeping of the feast of the Passover.

I want to give you proof that Jesus is the Passover Lamb and that His blood is the blood that sets us free. Jesus was set aside for observation and inspection five days before the sacrifice in the same way that the lamb was set aside for five days for inspection. In John 12:1 it says, *"Then, six days before the Passover, Jesus came to Bethany..."* Six days before the Passover Jesus showed up in Bethany where Lazarus was, whom He had raised from the dead. During this time religious leaders were trying to kill Lazarus because Jesus raised him from the dead. Jesus was at Lazarus' home six days before the Passover. Since the Passover was celebrated on the 14th, that means Jesus was in Bethany on the 9th. Then if you look at John 12:12,13, it says,

The next day a great multitude that had come to the feast, when they heard that Jesus was coming to Jerusalem,

took branches of palm trees and went out to meet Him, and cried out: "Hosanna! 'Blessed *is* He who comes in the name of the LORD!' The King of Israel!"

John 12:12,13

So the next day was the tenth which was the day of the triumphant entry into Jerusalem. From that point until the 14th, Jesus was scrutinized, questioned and interrogated to find out who He was. In fact, in Matthew 21:23-27, Jesus was questioned severely concerning His authority. In Matthew 23, they tried to trick Jesus. They tried to ask Him trick questions to get Him to say something that was wrong. But Jesus passed every single test. The scripture says He answered them perfectly. Finally, in desperation, when they couldn't find anything wrong with the Lamb of God, they sent Him to the Roman governor, Pilate. Look at what happened there in John chapter 19.

Pilate then went out again, and said to them, "Behold, I am bringing Him out to you, that you may know that I find no fault in Him."

John 19:4

The Jews couldn't find any fault in Jesus, so they turned Him over to the government. The government could not find any fault in Him either. The Lamb had been examined for five days and He was found without spot or blemish or fault. WOW! First Peter 1:18,19 says,

knowing that you were not redeemed with corruptible things, *like* silver or gold, from your aimless conduct *received* by tradition from your fathers,

but with the precious blood of Christ, as of a lamb without blemish and without spot.

1 Peter 1:18,19

The Lamb of God

OLD TESTAMENT *Sacrifice of Lambs*	NEW TESTAMENT *Sacrifice of the Lamb of God*
10th day of month of Nisan — lambs set aside for inspection	10th day of month of Nisan — Jesus entered Jerusalem
Lamb observed & tested for 5 days	Leaders observed & questioned the authority of Jesus for 5 days
Lamb to be spotless — with no fault	Pilate found no fault in Jesus
Prepared for death 9 am on 14th day of Nisan	Jesus nailed to cross 9 am on 14th day of Nisan
Lambs killed 3 pm on 14th day of Nisan	Jesus died 3 pm on 14th day of Nisan
Blood applied to the door posts of house	Jesus' blood was on Himself and He became the door
No bones broken	No bones broken
Whole lamb consumed by 6 pm	Body laid in tomb by 6pm
Blood of lambs saved Israelites from the angel of death	Blood of Jesus saves us from eternal death

The blood of Jesus was like the blood of an inspected sacrificial lamb. It was without blemish and without spot. Jesus was the Passover Lamb. Not only was He inspected like the Passover lamb for five days, but He was crucified and slaughtered on the same day and at the same time the Passover lambs were being sacrificed all over Jerusalem.

Jesus knew what was going on. He was not oblivious to this whole thing. In fact, in Matthew 26:2 you'll find where He said,

> **You know that after two days is the Passover, and the Son of Man will be delivered up to be crucified.**
>
> **Matthew 26:2**

Jesus knew exactly what was happening. He knew the exact day He was going to be crucified.

A Little History

Josephus, a first century Jewish historian, had this comment to make about the year Jesus was crucified. He said that in Jerusalem, the day Jesus was crucified, there were approximately 256,500 lambs slaughtered. That year the lambs were prepared at 9:00 a.m. on the morning of the 14th. They were prepared at 9:00 a.m. and they were killed at 3:00 p.m. so that everything could be completed by 6:00 p.m. At the exact time that the Jews were preparing their lambs, Jesus was being nailed to the cross. I've always wondered why these times in the Bible were mentioned. Why is it important to us what time of day it was? Here's the reason. Everything in the Word of God has a purpose. Everything in the Word of God has a reason. Everything is there, not by accident, but with great purpose.

Every Word in the Word Has a Purpose

One day I asked Charles Capps a question that had been puzzling me for a long time. When Simon Peter pulled in the net full of fish in John 21, why did John say there were 153 fish? John wrote this many years later. He didn't write it that day. Years later when John wrote down the account of what happened when Peter pulled in the fish, he said there were 153 fish. Once I thought to myself, "Who cares whether there were 153 or 161 or 82? If it was a big catch, that's all that matters. Right?" Wrong! There is a purpose to everything in the Word of God.

So one day while we were at the Lee C. Fine Airport and we were just yacking, I asked Charles, "Do you have any idea why there were 153 fish in the catch of fish recorded in the Book of John?" He said, "Well, I used to wonder that myself. But I was reading one day that in the sea where they were fishing there were 153 species of fish." When Bro. Capps made that statement, I thought to myself, "What a miracle! When Peter pulled out the net, it would have been a great shock if there weren't any two fish the same. Why else would they have counted them? I've seen bass fisherman that have won tournaments that can't tell you how many fish they had in their cooler and John remembered precisely years later because it was important.

They Crucified Him at the Third Hour

In Mark 15:25 it says, *"Now it was the third hour, and they crucified Him."* The third hour is 9:00 a.m. At 3:00 p.m. as the people were slaughtering the lambs, Jesus died. Mark was extremely careful to note the time as the ninth hour when Jesus breathed His last breath. It is recorded in Mark 15:33-37.

And it was the third hour (about nine o'clock in the morning) when they crucified Him.

Mark 15:25 (AMP)

Now when the sixth hour had come, there was darkness over the whole land until the ninth hour.

And at the ninth hour Jesus cried out with a loud voice, saying, "Eloi, Eloi, lama sabachthani?" which is translated, "My God, My God, why have You forsaken Me?"

Some of those who stood by, when they heard *that*, said, "Look, He is calling for Elijah!"

Then someone ran and filled a sponge full of sour wine, put *it* on a reed, and offered *it* to Him to drink, saying, "Let Him alone; let us see if Elijah will come to take Him down."

And Jesus cried out with a loud voice, and breathed His last.

Mark 15:33-37

Here's something else that proves Jesus was the Passover Lamb. The lamb was not to have any broken bones. When they were to prepare the lamb, one of the things that was very important was that the lamb was not to have any bones broken whatsoever. John 19:31 says, *"Therefore, because it was the Preparation Day, that the bodies should not remain on the cross on the Sabbath (for that Sabbath was a high day), the Jews asked Pilate that their legs might be broken, and that they might be taken away."*

Crucifixions were horrible. Sometimes they would crucify thousands at a time. It was a horrible thing!

They were attached to the crosses with nails. Because of the weight of their bodies and the way they were on the cross, it was extremely important that their legs and feet have a firm foundation. As their bodies would sag, it would cause their chest cavity to contract in such a way that they couldn't breathe. In order to breathe, they would push themselves up to take a breath and then they would drop back down. Just before they would die of suffocation, they would push themselves back up again and take another breath. When the Word said Jesus breathed His last, it wasn't just recording the fact that He stopped breathing. The Word was revealing prophecy.

Not One Bone Was Broken

Here's what happened. The next day was the Sabbath. It started at 6:00 p.m. that evening. The Jews did not want to leave the crucified bodies hanging on the crosses after 6:00 p.m. If they hadn't removed the bodies from the crosses before 6:00 p.m. (the beginning of the next day), they couldn't take them off until a day later. So, the Jews asked Pilate, "Would you break the legs of the Jews being crucified?" With their legs broken, they wouldn't be able to push themselves up and take the breath that would sustain their life. They would suffocate, literally strangle to death on the cross. That's what the Jews asked of Pilate.

Then the soldiers came and broke the legs of the first and of the other who was crucified with Him.

John 19:32

In other words, the soldiers went to the first thief on the cross and broke his legs. He dropped down, and because he could no longer raise himself to take a breath of air, he strangled and died. They then went to the second thief and broke his legs also. Then they approached Jesus and that takes us to verse 33.

But when they came to Jesus and saw that He was already dead, they did not break His legs.

John 19:33

Prophecy fulfilled! The sacrificial Lamb had no bones broken. Jesus was the perfect sacrificial Lamb, dying once and for all for your sins.

> **For these things were done that the Scripture should be fulfilled, "Not one of His bones shall be broken."**
>
> **John 19:36**

> **In one house it shall be eaten; you shall not carry any of the flesh outside the house, nor shall you break one of its bones.**
>
> **Exodus 12:46**

A Complete Sacrifice

The lamb was to be consumed and nothing left for the next day. The work must be finished. Jesus gave it all and nothing was left to be done the next day. He was removed from the cross like the lamb was removed from the spit crossbar.

When the lambs were roasted, the Hebrews used a spit with a crossbar and literally put the lamb up on the crossbar and spread it open so it could be roasted properly. Everything was to be off of the crossbar before the Sabbath started. The work had to be completed before the end of the day and the Jewish day ended at 6:00 p.m.

Jesus Became the Door

If you have gone to a Spirit filled church any time at all, you have heard John 10:10 quoted many times. *"The thief comes for no other reason except to steal, to kill and to destroy."* Jesus said it. It's in red letters in your Bible. He goes on to say, *"but I have come that they may have life and have it more abundantly."*

But let's back up one verse and look at John 10:9. In John 10:9 Jesus said, *"I am the door. If anyone enters by Me he will be saved."* Jesus had His own blood on Himself. We enter through Him into salvation, healing, prosperity and all the blessings of God. In the same way that the blood was put over the doorposts and the lintel and the Hebrews entered in through it with their family and possessions, today we must enter through Jesus. When the Hebrews were on the inside, they were saved. When the death angel came to their house, He backed off and went over it because of the blood. Jesus said no man comes to the Father except by Me. You can not get into the kingdom of God without going through the door (Jesus) of salvation. Remember Jesus said in John 10:9, *"I am the door."*

His Blood Was Shed Seven Ways

Because of the blood He sweat in the Garden of Gethsemane, because of the thorns pressed into His head, because of the internal bleeding from His bruises, because of the cut flesh on His back, because of the spear that was thrust into His side, because of nails in His hands and feet and because we enter through Him into salvation, we are passing through the Door covered with the redeeming blood of our Savior. We enter through Him (the door) and His blood is on Himself.

What was protected when the Hebrews went inside with the blood of the lambs on the doorposts? First of all, their lives. They didn't die. Second, their livestock. Third, their possessions were protected from the destroyer.

Better Promises Built on a Better Covenant

The old covenant was good and it has promises built on it, but the Word says the new covenant is better with better promises built on it. There was a flaw in the old covenant, so God brought us a better one.

The old covenant in Malachi chapter three is great. God said if you withhold your tithes and offerings, you are robbing Him. Then He goes on to say that if we bring all the tithes into the storehouse, that He will rebuke the devourer.

> **"Will a man rob God? Yet you have robbed Me! But you say, 'In what way have we robbed You?' In tithes and offerings.**
>
> **"You are cursed with a curse, For you have robbed Me, *Even* this whole nation.**
>
> **"Bring all the tithes into the storehouse, That there may be food in My house, And try Me now in this," Says the LORD of hosts, "If I will not open for you the windows of heaven And pour out for you such blessing That there will not be room enough to receive it.**
>
> **"And I will rebuke the devourer for your sakes, So that he will not destroy the fruit of your ground, Nor shall the vine fail to bear fruit for you in the field," Says the LORD of hosts.**
>
> **Malachi 3:8-11**

That is a great promise. If we'll bring all the tithes into the storehouse, God will rebuke the devourer. But that's under the old covenant. It's not bad, but it's an old covenant promise. How could it be any better? Let me explain to you how much better it gets.

Under the new covenant Jesus gave us His blood, He gave us His name and He gave us His Word. *He gave us the authority to rebuke the devil ourselves.* Under the old covenant, you do what you are supposed to do and God will rebuke the devourer. While you are waiting for Him to rebuke the devourer, you may think, "Come on! Come on! It's rebuking time. Come on, God!" Under the new covenant we are not to wait for God to rebuke the devourer. God is waiting for us to act on the authority He has given as a result of the blood. God has given you the name of Jesus and the power and authority to do it yourself. When the devil gets in your face, you say, "I rebuke you devil in the name of Jesus."

Jesus said to say to that mountain, *"be removed and be cast into the sea."* Many times in the Bible the word "mountain" means kingdom. Under the old covenant you did what you were supposed to do, then you waited for God to move the mountain (kingdom). Under the new covenant Jesus said, *"Say to the mountain 'be removed and cast into the sea' and believe in your heart that those things you say will come to pass and you will have whatever you say."*

To me it's a greater covenant and a greater promise, but with every greater promise comes greater responsibility. Under the old covenant you do what you are supposed to do and just wait for God. Under the new covenant you do what you are supposed to do, take authority yourself and stand in faith without wavering.

Malachi chapter three is not a bad promise and in no way am I belittling it. I thank God for it. However, the better promise is in the new covenant. Don't allow spiritual laziness to rob you of the best promise.

The Serpent on a Pole

> **"And as Moses lifted up the serpent in the wilderness, even so must the Son of Man be lifted up,**
>
> **"that whoever believes in Him should not perish but have eternal life."**
>
> **John 3:14,15**

While the Hebrews were in the wilderness, they were bitten by fiery serpents. Snakes were biting them and they were dying. When Moses asked God for help, God told him to go to the edge of the camp and put up a pole. On top of the pole, he was to put an image of a bronze serpent. Then they were given instructions for life.

When someone was bitten by a fiery serpent or snake, they were to look up at the bronze serpent. Then they wouldn't die, they would live.

First of all they had to do it by faith. They had to believe that God really meant what He said. They could have stayed on the other side of the camp and said, "We don't believe it." If they did that, they would die. But if they were obedient, they would go to the pole of the bronze serpent, look and live. The serpent on a pole has become the icon for the modern medical profession. You can see it displayed on clinics, doctor's offices and hospitals around the world.

Making an Icon out of a Move of God

We must be careful that we don't take the things of God that are powerful and make them into religious icons. In some churches you only hear about the power of the blood of Jesus on the week of Passover. Rarely do we hear in depth teachings about the birth of Jesus unless it's Christmas. Likewise, we rarely hear sermons about His resurrection unless it's Resurrection Day. These teachings are not seasonal. They are foundational.

For some reason religious man has always attempted to make icons out of the things of God . Four hundred years after God told Moses to put the bronze serpent at the edge of the camp, during the time of King Hezekiah, people were worshiping the same bronze serpent. It had become a religious symbol. They even gave it a name: Nehushtan. Godly traditions are good, but traditions created from the mind of man will only cause separation from the Truth of God. The Hebrews had taken a plan of God for the moment and when the moment had passed, they turned the good plan into a false doctrine. When God delivers us out of a trial, we must move past the deliverance and into His next plan

He has for us. If we continue to worship the "serpent on the pole," we will never move into the fullness of our own ministry.

Don't let the Passover and the blood of Jesus and the fact that Jesus was the sacrificial Lamb that was slain for you so that you can have deliverance under the new covenant become an "Easter" thing. Don't get confused. The blood of Jesus is a daily reality that brings life to the believer. Revelation 12:11 says, *"And they overcame him* (talking about the devil) *by the blood of the Lamb and the Word of their testimony."*

How to Become a Christian

There is only one way to have everlasting life. There is only one way to live forever and be assured that you will always be with the Lord. There is only one way to the kingdom of God and the kingdom of heaven. There is only one way to the Father and that one way is Jesus.

God loved you so much that He sent Jesus to earth to pay the price for your sins and make a way for you to live forever with Him. He paid the price you could not pay. He made a way of escape from the bondage of sin and death.

Receiving the gift of salvation is simple. It basically involves five steps. Read these steps and the scriptures. Then pray and accept the gift of salvation.

Step #1
You Must Believe in Jesus

For God so loved the world that He gave His only begotten Son, that whoever believes in Him should not perish but have everlasting life.

For God did not send His Son into the world to condemn the world, but that the world through Him might be saved.

John 3:16,17

Believe on the Lord Jesus Christ, and you will be saved, you and your household.

Acts 16:31

Step #2
You Must Confess Your Sins

You must acknowledge that you are a sinner and you want Jesus to wash your sins away.

If we confess our sins, He is faithful and just to forgive us our sins and to cleanse us from all unrighteousness.

1 John 1:9

Step #3
You Must Repent
(turn away from your sins)

For the wages of sin is death, but the gift of God is eternal life in Christ Jesus our Lord.

Romans 6:23

The time is fulfilled, and the kingdom of God is at hand. Repent and believe in the gospel.

Mark 1:15

Step #4
You Must Confess Jesus Before Men

If you confess with your mouth the Lord Jesus and believe in your heart that God has raised Him from the dead, you will be saved.

For with the heart one believes unto righteousness, and with the mouth confession is made unto salvation.

Romans 10:9,10

Step #5
You Must Accept the Gift of Salvation

For by grace you have been saved through faith, and that not of yourselves; it is the gift of God.

Ephesians 2:8

But as many as received Him, to them He gave the right to become children of God, to those who believe in His name.

John 1:12

Behold, now is the accepted time; behold, now is the day of salvation.

2 Corinthians 6:2

Dear Heavenly Father,

I come in the Name of Jesus. I thank You for sending Your Son, Jesus, into this world to die for my sins and for raising Him from the dead so that I can have everlasting life.

I recognize and acknowledge Jesus as my Savior and as the Lord of my life. I repent of my sins and I forgive those who have wronged me. I believe in my heart and I will confess openly my belief in Jesus.

Thank You for forgiving me of my sins and giving me eternal life. I receive this gift by faith,

In Jesus' name,
Amen

"I say to you that likewise there will be more joy in heaven over one sinner who repents than over ninety-nine just persons who need no repentance."

— Jesus
Luke 15:7

For ministry information contact:

Larry Ollison Ministries
P.O. Box 880
Osage Beach, MO 65065
(573) 348-9777

e-mail: office@ollison.org
website: www.ollison.org

Other Books by Larry Ollison:

Discover the Power of Grace in Righteousness
God's Plan For Handling Stress
Is Faith Really Important?

About the Author

Larry Ollison has been in the ministry for over 30 years. Raised a Southern Baptist and majoring in theology at Southwest Baptist University, Larry now ministers to all denominations through the gifts of the Holy Spirit.

Larry is the author of several books and articles. His weekly newspaper column is read by thousands.

Larry is a Director for *International Convention of Faith Ministries* and Vice President of *Spirit FM Christian Radio Network.* He is also the host of *The Cutting Edge* radio broadcast that airs three times daily. Other ministries include Bibles Behind Bars and TIPI Ministries (an outreach ministry to Native Americans).

Larry is Pastor of *Walk on the Water Faith Church,* Founder and President of *Faith Bible Training Center,* a member of *Who's Who Worldwide* and on the board of several corporations and ministries.

Larry is a pastor, pilot, teacher, and author. His number one goal is to meet the needs of the people through the teaching of faith in God's Word.